HORSES

The origins and characteristics of 100 breeds

HORSES

The origins and characteristics of 100 breeds

MOIRA C. HARRIS • NICOLA JANE SWINNEY

METRO BOOKS

NEW YORK

WELDON OWEN PTY LTD
Managing Director Kay Scarlett
Publisher Corinne Roberts
Creative Director Sue Burk
Art Manager Trucie Henderson
Senior Vice President, International Sales Stuart Laurence
Sales Manager: North America Ellen Towell
Vice President Sales: Asia and Latin America Dawn L. Owen
Administration Manager, International Sales Kristine Ravn
Production Director Todd Rechner
Production and Prepress Controller Mike Crowton
Production Controller Lisa Conway
Production Coordinator Nathan Grice

Editor Lachlan McLaine
Designer John Bull, The Book Design Company
Picture Research Joanna Collard
Index Puddingburn Publishing Services
Editorial Assistant Natalie Ryan

Metro Books
122 Fifth Avenue
New York, NY 10011

ISBN: 978-1-4351-2724-1

Color reproduction by Chroma Graphics (Overseas) Pte Ltd
Printed by Tien Wah Press, Malaysia
Manufactured in Malaysia
10 9 8 7 6 5 4 3 2 1

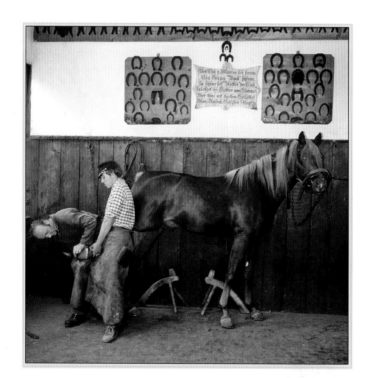

Contents

THE BREEDS

ORIGINS

ARABIAN INFLUENCE

SPANISH INFLUENCE

WARMBLOODS

THE AMERICAS

FOREWORD

From the time, thousands of years ago, when our ancestors stopped thinking of the horse as food and saw it instead as a loyal worker in field and forest and a means to traverse great distances, the horse has walked beside us, calm and unprotesting, as we have spread forth across the globe.

The horse has played a vital role in the growth and evolution of almost every country on Earth. From the barren deserts of Arabia to the peat fields and tin mines of England; from the steppes and mountains of Mongolia to the vast plains of the Americas—the horse has been there. It has gone to war with us, crossed the seas with us, and toiled in the heat and the cold with us. And always without complaint.

As the world changed—so much of its development and growth borne from its industry—our need for the horse as a working partner has waned. But our fascination with, and love for, this glorious creature has never died.

This book is a celebration of the beauty and spirit of the horse and our unique partnership with this animal. At its heart is a survey of 100 horse breeds from around the world. Some of these breeds are entirely the product of the environment in which they have lived for hundreds or thousands of years. However, the vast majority are the result of the guiding hand of generations of horse breeders, each in search of a horse ideally suited to its purpose.

Thus, each breed has a story to tell from our shared history and throws a different light on the part that the horse has played, and continues to play, in the human story.

How to Use this Book

This book has two main sections. The first section, "Themes," provides an overview of the horse: the nature of the animal, the role it has played in human history, horses in art and legend, and the place horses have in the modern world. The second, much larger, section is "The Breeds." Here, 100 of the world's most important horse and pony breeds are surveyed in detail using text, maps, tables, and photographs. The breeds are organized into eight chapters depending on their place of origin and genealogy.

Themes PAGES 12–31

Text, illustrations, graphics, and photographs are combined to provide a close look at a particular aspect of horse history, biology, or involvement with the human world.

The Breeds PAGES 32–233

The 100 breeds featured in The Breeds section are organized into eight chapters.

ORIGINS

Of the three, possibly four, subspecies thought to be the foundation of all the breeds extant today, Przewalski's Horse is the only survivor. The Arab, too, is an ancient breed, and has had a major influence on the modern horse. This chapter looks at the oldest known horse and pony breeds and their links with today's breeds.

ARABIAN INFLUENCE

The Arab has, perhaps more than any other breed, played a major role in the development of the modern horse, and its beauty can be seen throughout the world's equines. The links between the Arab and other breeds are explored in this chapter.

SPANISH INFLUENCE

The Iberian breeds, including the Andalusian, Lusitano, Alter-Real, and Sorraia, have had a far-reaching influence, including the famous white horses of Vienna, the Royal horses of Denmark, and the hardy ponies of England, as this chapter explains.

WARMBLOODS

Warmblood—literally, a mix of hotblood, such as Arab or Thoroughbred, and coldblood, such as a draft breed—is a

modern success story. This chapter looks at the Warmblood breeds—today's premier competition horses.

THE AMERICAS

Most horses in the Americas are Spanish in origin, brought to the New World by the Conquistadors of the sixteenth century. This chapter examines the range of the modern North and South American breeds, from the tiny Falabella to the charismatic Paso Fino and iconic Mustang.

PONIES

Great Britain and Ireland have a rich heritage of pony breeds, which are famed worldwide for their beauty, strength, and endurance. These breeds, in their turn, have influenced other equines all over the world.

WORLD BREEDS

Whatever country you may visit, you will find the horse—this chapter surveys the many and varied breeds found in India, Russia, Iceland, and beyond.

HEAVY BREEDS

From the days when a horse was required to carry a knight in full armor, the heavy—or draft—breeds have had a role to play. The heavy breeds are still revered the world over, as seen in this chapter.

THE FACTS TABLE

Essential details about the breed are presented in The Facts table. This provides at-a-glance information about significant aspects of each breed.

Origin
The country and often the region of origin

Color
The breed's usual coat color and patterns

Physique
Brief description of the body shape and proportions

Features
Special qualities of the breed

Use
Activities and sports to which the breed is suited

Height
Average height in hands (equal to 4 inches) and meters. Note that when a horse height is given with a point, it is to indicate inches in addition to the number of full hands, not a decimal fraction of a hand. Thus 16.2 hands equals 16 hands and 2 inches, or 66 inches.

Temperament
Brief summary of the temperament

THE FACTS

Origin	Austria
Color	predominantly gray
Height	16.2 hands (1.68 m)
Physique	neat head, short, muscular neck, flat wither, sloping shoulder, long back, strong legs
Features	long-lived, late-maturing, powerful
Temperament	intelligent, gentle, trainable
Use	classical equitation, riding, harness, dressage

Introduction
This text provides a detailed description of the breed, including its origins, history, and distinguishing characteristics.

Locator map
This map shows the geographical provenance of the breed with major towns and any important places in the breed's history identified.

Running head
The current chapter of The Breeds section is indicated in the running head on the right-hand page.

Global map
This shows in what part of the world the breed originated.

Ancestry chart
This chart details the genealogy of the breed.

Conformation photo
This shows a good example of the breed in profile. Relevant body features are labeled for further information.

Size comparison
The size of the horse is compared to an average adult male.

Photographs
Taken by leading equine photographers, these show the breed in context: at work, at rest, and in their natural environment.

Equine Evolution

The evolution of the horse is a 60-million-year story of change—from small to large, from four toes to one, from browser to grazer. The development of the equine species can be traced to a small animal known as *Eohippus,* which developed in North America and migrated to Europe. The first true horse appeared 1.5 million years ago, also in North America, and spread over land bridges to South America, Europe, Asia, and Africa. Horses became extinct in the Americas about 8,000 years ago and were reintroduced by the Spanish only in the sixteenth century. The horse was probably saved from extinction in Eurasia by the advent of domestication by humans. This is thought to have first occurred about 5,000 years ago on the shores of the Black and Caspian seas. Modern horses and ponies are believed to derive from three or four types: the Forest Horse, Prezewalski's Horse, the Tarpan, and possibly the Tundra Horse.

Lascaux horse
Drawings of prehistoric horses appear in the Lascaux caves of France. These artworks are around 16,000 years old.

The ridden horse
This rock carving in Utah depicts a hunter on horseback. It must date from after the reintroduction of the horse to North America in the sixteenth century.

From Four Toes to One
The forefeet of *Eohippus* had four toes. Over millennia, three toes became the norm with the central toe increasingly carrying the weight. *Pliohippus* was the first of the single-hoofed horses, and *Equus* retained this characteristic.

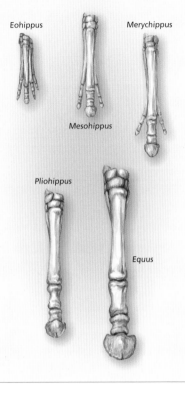

Eohippus

Merychippus

Mesohippus

Pliohippus

Equus

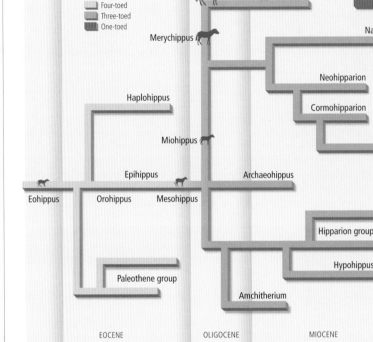

- Four-toed
- Three-toed
- One-toed

Equus
Dinohippus
Hippidion group
Pliohippus
Calippus
Nannipus
Merychippus
Neohipparion
Haplohippus
Cormohipparion
Miohippus
Stylohipparion
Epihippus
Archaeohippus
Eohippus
Orohippus
Mesohippus
Hipparion group
Hypohippus
Paleothene group
Amchitherium

PLIOCENE
PLEISTOCENE
PRESENT

EOCENE   OLIGOCENE   MIOCENE

55   36   27   5   2   0
Millions of years ago

Equine phylogeny
The modern horse developed over a period of 60 million years. Between *Eohippus* (or *Hyracotherium*) and *Equus*, many branches of the family tree died out.

The road to *Equus*
Fossil evidence illustrates the evolution of the horse from the 14-inch (35-cm) four-toed browsing animal of 60 million years ago, to a 48-inch (1.2-m), single-toed, grazing animal of 6 million years ago.

1 *Eohippus*
Originating in North America 60 million years ago, *Eohippus* had four toes on its front feet and three on its hind. The eyes were oriented to face forward rather than to the side, and the teeth were for browsing, not grazing.

HEIGHT
14 inches
(35 cm)

2 *Mesohippus*
By 35 to 40 million years ago, *Mesohippus* had increased in height and body weight. It still had padded feet, but now had three toes.

HEIGHT
18 inches
(45 cm)

Fossil foot
This fossilized horse hoof was found in Gran Dolina, an important archeological site in Spain. It dates from at least 150,000 years ago, when the human occupants of the cave hunted horses for their meat.

HEIGHT
48 inches
(1.2 m)

5 *Pliohippus*
Pliohippus was the first equine to have a single-toed hoof. It was probably the ancestor of the modern horse, the ass, and the zebra.

HEIGHT
36 inches
(90 cm)

4 **Merychippus**
Merychippus grew taller still, and increasingly its middle toe came to bear most of the weight. It lived 25 to 20 million years ago and was the first true grazer.

HEIGHT
24 inches
(60 cm)

3 *Miohippus*
Miohippus coexisted with *Mesohippus* for several million years. *Mesohippus* died out and *Miohippus* evolved, developing longer limbs and a longer skull, and losing its arched back.

Preserved in stone
Propalaeotherium hassiacum is descended from *Eohippus*, but this line died out early. This fossil from Germany has a remarkably complete skeleton, and even the flesh contours are visible.

SENSES AND BEHAVIOR

As a prey animal, a horse's complex blend of senses and instincts is largely concerned with defense against predators. It is armed with enough weaponry—teeth, hooves, and strength—that it can usually fend off a would-be attacker. However, the horse's main defense is its speed. In a domesticated horse, the "flight" response is seen when it is frightened, resulting in "shying" or "spooking" behavior. The horse's senses work together not only to protect it, but also to ensure that it thrives. Eyes are positioned on each side of the head, providing almost 360-degree vision. Acute hearing allows the horse to react to danger before it presents itself. The horse's sense of smell, its most developed sense, serves not only as a tool to recognize friend or foe, but aids in survival by locating water and sustenance.

SENSES

Hearing
A horse's ears can rotate nearly 180 degrees, which allows it to detect and identify sounds, determine where they are coming from, and run to safety if needed.

Smell
Its most keen sense, a horse's sense of smell allows a mare to identify her foal, locate water even underground, and allows stallions to detect a mare in season.

Sight
Horses have an excellent field of vision. While they are not color-blind, they do not process colors as humans do.

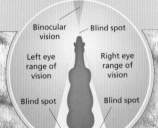

Binocular vision — Blind spot
Left eye range of vision — Right eye range of vision
Blind spot — Blind spot

BODY LANGUAGE

Bucking
A horse will buck in order to rid itself from something on its back. Horses will also buck and run exuberantly when they have excess energy.

Flehmen response
This is a lifting of the upper lip, which allows a horse to smell more acutely. Stallions display this response when smelling the urine of a mare in heat.

Pawing
Pawing indicates impatience, nervousness, or irritation. Stallions become hyperactive, alert, and restless before mating and can lift their legs high in the air.

Fighting
Combative horses will first posture and squeal to get their opponent to back down. If the fight is on, they will kick, bite, rear and lunge at each other.

Lead stallion
The stallion is in charge of keeping the band together as a unit and protecting it from predators. He will forcefully defend himself against other stallions seeking to usurp his position.

Touch

Receptive nerves under its coat allow a horse to feel the tiniest sensations, such as the presence of a fly. The sensitive muzzle compensates for a blind spot in front of its face.

Taste

Horses take pleasure from eating and will select food that is flavorful when presented a choice. They have a palate that prefers sweet over bitter. They often will reject water with an unfamiliar taste.

Bachelor band

Because horses are social creatures, older colts and young stallions must stick together in groups to survive. They form bachelor bands until they gather mares of their own.

The wild herd

Horses are highly social herd animals. In the wild, herds are comprised of tightly knit groups called bands. A band might consist of one stallion, a mare or harem of mares, and their foals. There is a social hierarchy within bands, which allows peaceful harmonious life. The hierarchy allows orderly access to limited resources, like the best forage, water, shade, and shelter.

Lead mare

The lead mare, sometimes called the boss mare or "alpha" mare, runs the band, directing it to safety, locating food and water, and controlling it when the stallion goes off on his own.

Mares and foals

Within the band a hierarchy is established among the mares and their foals. The pecking order will change whenever members leave or join the band.

ANATOMY AND PHYSIOLOGY

The horse is a non-ruminant herbivore, meaning it does not have a multi-compartmented stomach like a cow. Because they do not chew their cud, horses must spend 9 to 11 hours a day grazing—longer than other grass-eating ruminants. When not eating, horses rest; adult horses sleep for approximately four hours per day, with two of those hours standing. The gestation period is 11 months and, although twins are possible, usually only one foal survives unless there is human intervention. The horse is one of the fastest land mammals. The Quarter Horse can reach 47.5 miles per hour (76.4 km/h) when sprinting. While some horses are built for speed, others are for power. A team of two draft horses can pull a sled with a 2-ton (1.8 tonne) load.

HORSE TYPES

Light
Usually saddle horses, light breeds are used for riding and in some cases harness. Most are "hotblooded" or "warmblooded."

Heavy
Known as drafts, these animals are used for their immense strength and are generally not ridden. These are considered "coldblooded."

Pony
Ponies are small horses, under 14.2 hands (147 cm). Most ponies have body shapes that are proportionately different from full-sized horses.

INTERNAL ANATOMY

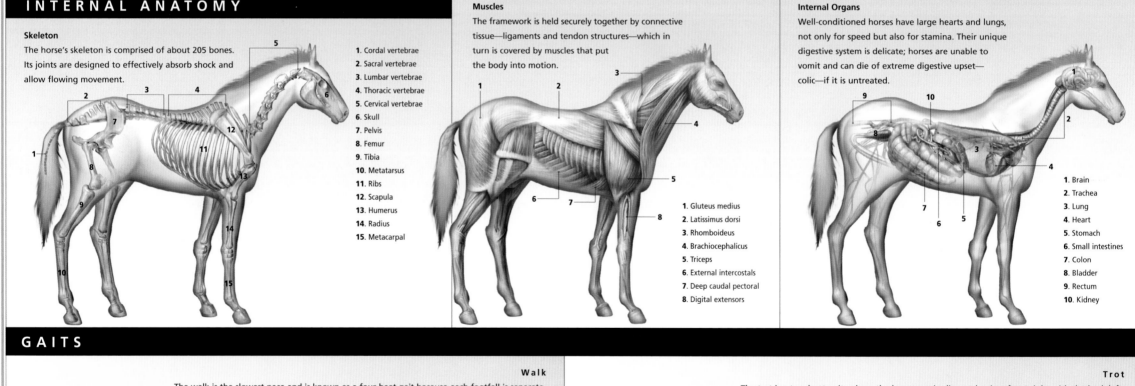

Skeleton
The horse's skeleton is comprised of about 205 bones. Its joints are designed to effectively absorb shock and allow flowing movement.

1. Cordal vertebrae
2. Sacral vertebrae
3. Lumbar vertebrae
4. Thoracic vertebrae
5. Cervical vertebrae
6. Skull
7. Pelvis
8. Femur
9. Tibia
10. Metatarsus
11. Ribs
12. Scapula
13. Humerus
14. Radius
15. Metacarpal

Muscles
The framework is held securely together by connective tissue—ligaments and tendon structures—which in turn is covered by muscles that put the body into motion.

1. Gluteus medius
2. Latissimus dorsi
3. Rhomboideus
4. Brachiocephalicus
5. Triceps
6. External intercostals
7. Deep caudal pectoral
8. Digital extensors

Internal Organs
Well-conditioned horses have large hearts and lungs, not only for speed but also for stamina. Their unique digestive system is delicate; horses are unable to vomit and can die of extreme digestive upset—colic—if it is untreated.

1. Brain
2. Trachea
3. Lung
4. Heart
5. Stomach
6. Small intestines
7. Colon
8. Bladder
9. Rectum
10. Kidney

GAITS

Walk
The walk is the slowest pace and is known as a four-beat gait because each footfall is separate.

Trot
The trot is a two-beat gait, where the legs move in diagonal pairs—front right with the back left, and front left with the back right.

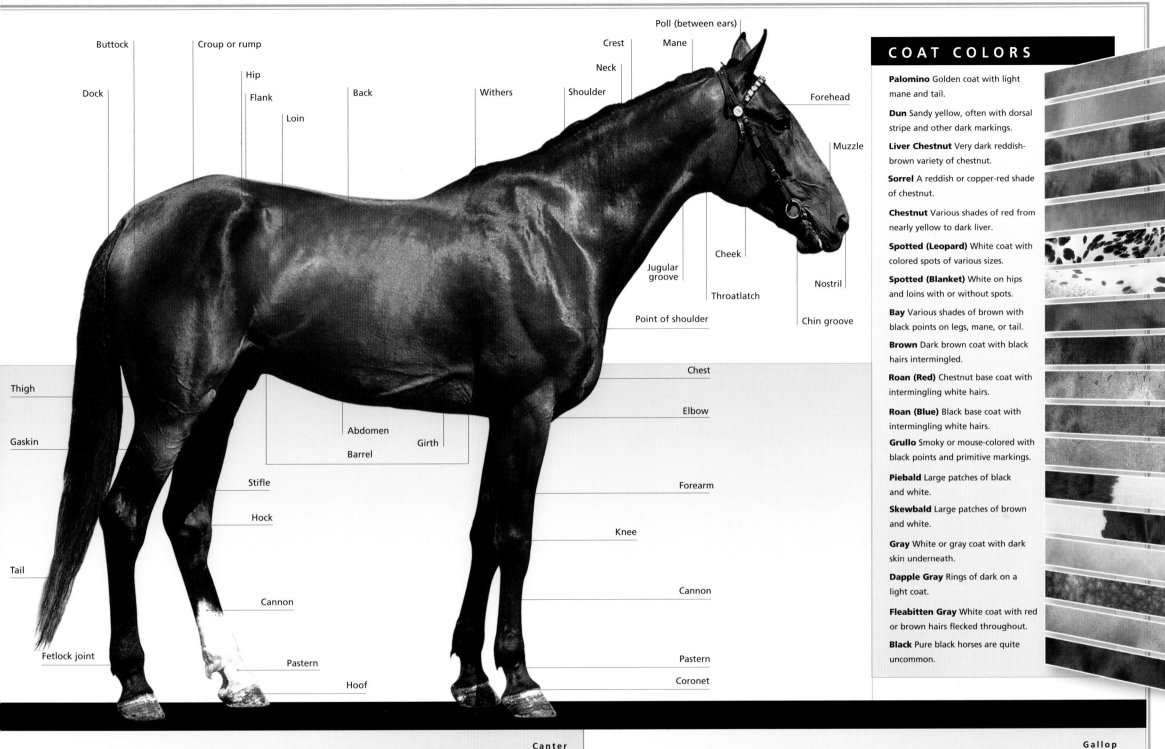

Buttock

Croup or rump

Hip

Dock

Flank

Back

Loin

Poll (between ears)

Crest

Mane

Neck

Withers

Shoulder

Forehead

Muzzle

Cheek

Jugular groove

Nostril

Throatlatch

Chin groove

Point of shoulder

Thigh

Chest

Elbow

Gaskin

Abdomen

Girth

Barrel

Stifle

Forearm

Hock

Knee

Tail

Cannon

Cannon

Fetlock joint

Pastern

Pastern

Hoof

Coronet

COAT COLORS

Palomino Golden coat with light mane and tail.

Dun Sandy yellow, often with dorsal stripe and other dark markings.

Liver Chestnut Very dark reddish-brown variety of chestnut.

Sorrel A reddish or copper-red shade of chestnut.

Chestnut Various shades of red from nearly yellow to dark liver.

Spotted (Leopard) White coat with colored spots of various sizes.

Spotted (Blanket) White on hips and loins with or without spots.

Bay Various shades of brown with black points on legs, mane, or tail.

Brown Dark brown coat with black hairs intermingled.

Roan (Red) Chestnut base coat with intermingling white hairs.

Roan (Blue) Black base coat with intermingling white hairs.

Grullo Smoky or mouse-colored with black points and primitive markings.

Piebald Large patches of black and white.

Skewbald Large patches of brown and white.

Gray White or gray coat with dark skin underneath.

Dapple Gray Rings of dark on a light coat.

Fleabitten Gray White coat with red or brown hairs flecked throughout.

Black Pure black horses are quite uncommon.

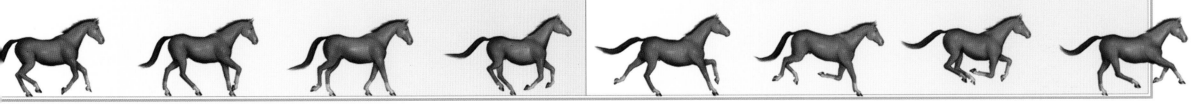

Canter

The canter is a three-beat gait. A cantering horse appears as though it is skipping to the right or left. The direction is determined by which leg the horse leads with.

Gallop

The gallop is like a very fast canter, except there are four footfalls to its beat. At one point during the gallop, all feet will be off the ground.

DOMESTICATION AND TRAINING

Horses were originally hunted by humans for their meat. When some later neolithic people took up a settled farming existence, they tamed horses in herds to make them manageable and compliant. This probably first occurred about 5,000 to 6,000 years ago. But when humans discovered that the horse could be trained and ridden, their role changed dramatically. A domesticated horse could be used as a beast of burden, as an aid to hunting, or as a means to traverse long distances. Cultures that mastered horsemanship were able to conquer their neighbors and horses soon became central to warfare. By the middle of the second millennium B.C., chariot and cavalry horses were used throughout Greece, Egypt, Mesopotamia, and China. Today, perhaps 8,000 years after the first horse was tamed, horse training remains a valued skill.

Sumerian war chariots (above)
From as early as 2800 B.C., armies were making use of the horse as a weapon of war. This detail from an ancient Sumerian mosaic inlaid box is one of the earliest known portrayals of domesticated equines. It is believed to show asses pulling war chariots.

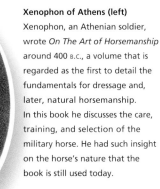

Xenophon of Athens (left)
Xenophon, an Athenian soldier, wrote *On The Art of Horsemanship* around 400 B.C., a volume that is regarded as the first to detail the fundamentals for dressage and, later, natural horsemanship. In this book he discusses the care, training, and selection of the military horse. He had such insight on the horse's nature that the book is still used today.

Golden chariot (below)
The horse and chariot made its way into Egypt relatively late in its history, around 1500 B.C. Egyptian chariots were pulled by a pair of horses, and were used in war, hunting, and in ceremony. Horses were considered a sign of prestige and wealth. They lived in fine stables, and received excellent care and feed—better than many people.

Terracotta army and horses (left)
China's warhorses of the Qin Dynasty (211–206 B.C.) pulled two-wheeled chariots and a single warrior into battle. But they were also used under saddle. The Chinese have been credited with creating the horseshoe, to make the hoof more durable, and the stirrup, to bring comfort and stability in riding.

Greece

For the Greeks, the horse embodied speed and competition. During the sixth century B.C., the ruling families in Athens expressed their appreciation by beginning or ending their name with *hippos*, the Greek word for horse. This marble and bronze bust originally decorated the Mausoleum at Halikarnassos.

Britain

Britain's Iron Age people must have held their horses in high regard because their harnesses and carts were among the most highly decorated objects created by that culture. Pictured left is a selection of bronze and glass harness pieces from several locations.

Iran

This bronze horse bit dates from between 1000 and 700 B.C. It was taken from a grave site in western Iran where some of the oldest breeds of horse were developed.

TRAINING

Training a horse ideally starts when it is still a juvenile. A colt or filly will be trained to give to the pressure of a headcollar (halter) and lead; it will learn to accept its trainer as the "lead horse." When it matures for riding, at about three years of age for the saddle horse, it will become accustomed to saddle and bridle before a rider sits astride. A horse may be "long-lined" which allows it to understand cues from the bit while a handler walks behind the horse. Finally, the rider will mount the horse and begin to teach the horse it respond to leg and seat cues.

Horses respond well to positive reinforcement, repetitive training, and praise, whether verbal or physical. They also remember negative training, so trainers must take care that they are patient and consistent in order to produce a quality riding horse.

Jerez de la Frontera equestrian school

The Real Escuela Andaluza del Arte Ecuestre in Jerez de la Frontera, Spain, is dedicated to preserving the Andalusian horse breed as well as promoting and maintaining the baroque style of classical dressage.

Breaking in a filly

Trainers who practice natural horsemanship methods understand the nature of horses and herd mentality. Using equine psychology and communication techniques similar to those used by horses in the wild, they are able to partner with the horse in a non-abusive manner. This training attempts to keep the horse feeling safe and calm throughout the process, and rewards any positive reaction toward the goal.

THE HORSE AT WORK

The very word horsepower is synonymous with strength, and for hundreds of years the horse was the primary and most versatile source of power in the world. Specially bred heavy horses were used for tilling, plowing, logging, transporting goods, and drawing floats and drays. Lighter horses transported passengers, from luxury coaches to practical hansom cabs. Ponies carried a successful day's hunt from the mountain, or coal from underground mines. The horse helped move civilization into modern times and, although the machine has mostly replaced the working horse, there are many places around the world where they are still an everyday sight.

A *London Cab*, c.1845, Charles Cooper Henderson
Life was not easy for the nineteenth-century urban cab horse. The rise in city populations increased the demand for passenger transport. Cab operations were big business, and owners generally wanted to get the most out of their charges. As well as intense traffic congestion, meager food, and long hours in harness, horses were often worked very hard—sometimes to death.

Unloading ice (below right)
For centuries horse-drawn vehicles were essential for commerce, as common a sight as trucks and vans are on today's roads. This illustration from 1911 shows ice being unloaded at a dock. The horse is eating from a nosebag, which allowed it to refuel on the go.

THE MEDIEVAL AGRICULTURAL HORSE

Detail from *Landscape with the Fall of Icarus*, c.1555, Pieter Bruegel the Elder
Peasants of the Middle Ages lived and worked on land owned by local lords. In exchange they gave their labor and paid rent in cash or some of the food they produced. A peasant family was unlikely to be able to afford to own or keep a horse, but a village might pool together to buy one or two and then rotate their use. Here, a single horse pulls a simple plow.

Fifteenth century English painting, unknown artist
The most common tools used by medieval farmers were metal-tipped plows for turning over the soil and harrows to cover up the soil after seeds had been planted. This scene shows horses at work, but oxen were a more common working farm animal.

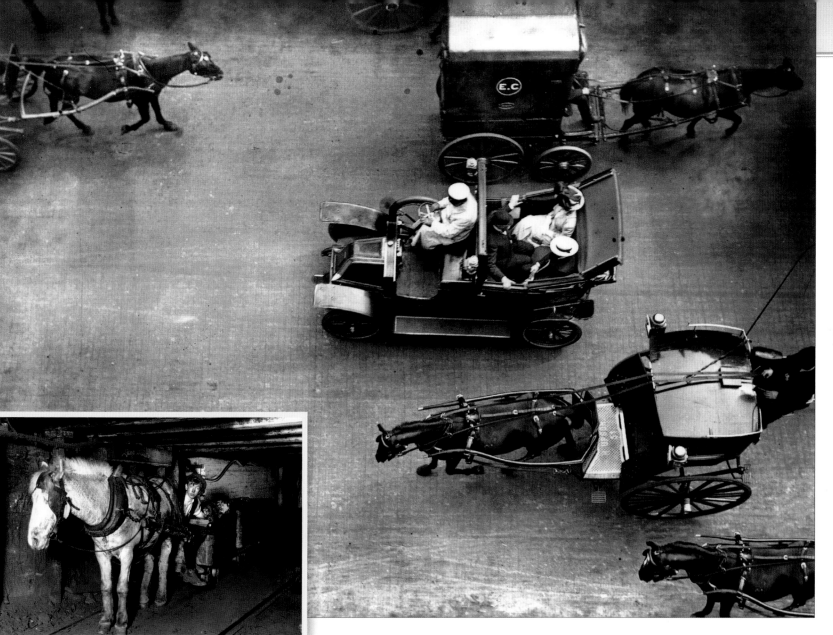

Changing traffic (left)

Horse-drawn carriages and carts dominate this London street scene from about 1905. But a new vehicle has made an appearance: the motor car. This marked the beginning of the end for the age of horse-drawn transport. But for several decades to come, horses and automobiles shared the roads.

Pit pony (left inset)

Thousands of ponies worked and lived in coal mines from the mid-eighteenth up until the mid-twentieth century. Known as pit ponies, these small, hardy equines hauled coal through the network of underground shafts and came up to the surface only when the pit was closed for holidays, or when their working days were over.

Canal horse (below left)

Horses working the canals were known as "boaters." They were powerful, yet small and compact enough to fit under bridges and navigate narrow pathways, known as towpaths.

WORKING HORSES TODAY

Although many jobs that horses once held are today performed by machine, horses still can be found hard at work both in developed and developing countries. They are used in harness tilling the land, bringing incrops, logging, and as pack animals. For the South American gauchos, the North American cowboy, and the Australian drover, horses are still the preferred mode of transport in areas inaccessible by even all-terrain vehicles.

THE HORSE AT WAR

For as long as people have had command of horses they have been used to wage war. Many—perhaps most—innovations in equine training methods, equipment, and breeding resulted from a perennial arms race between armies using chariots and cavalry. One of the earliest texts on horsemanship was written in 1345 B.C., by Kikkuli, a Hittite horseman. It describes the care and training of the warhorse. Some 1,000 years later, Xenophon, an Athenian soldier, wrote *On The Art of Horsemanship*, a foundation for classical riding that is still consulted today. Classical dressage has its origins in exercises to develop the military horse and rider. Even in the age of mechanized warfare, horses and mules were used extensively in transport and logistics roles. Today, military horses are mostly used for ceremonial purposes and for reconnaissance and border patrols.

Ancient Egypt
The ancient Egyptians used horses to pull chariots as early as 3000 B.C. The speed and mobility of the chariot had a significant impact on battle tactics. This detail from an inlaid box shows a warrior king defeating an army of black Africans.

Alexander the Great
There are many legends regarding Alexander the Great (356–323 B.C.), King of Macedon and conqueror of much of Asia. At age ten, he was said to have tamed Bucephalus, a great black horse that no one else could subdue. This bas-relief carving depicts Alexander (left) astride Bucephalus fighting the Persians at the Battle of Issus, 333 B.C.

Medieval battle
A knight on horseback was by far the most powerful and feared soldier of the Middle Ages. A knight's warhorse had to be strong, brave, and nimble. Along with his armor and his sword, his warhorse was a knight's most valuable possession. A good warhorse could cost 20 times as much as a regular horse, and many knights had more than one.

THE ARMORED HORSE

By the late Middle Ages, both warhorse and rider were protected with elaborate plate armor made from hammered steel. This armor was incredibly expensive; only men from the richest families could become knights.

Chaffron
The most important piece of horse armor was the chaffron, which protected the horse's face.

END OF AN ERA

The First World War was the last major conflict in which mounted cavalry played an important role, primarily on the Eastern Front and in the Middle East. But trench warfare with barbed wire and massed machine guns largely put an end to the tactic of the cavalry charge. Horses on the Western Front were mostly deployed for transportation and hauling artillery. Horses and mules were used in such large numbers that the war significantly reduced the world's equine population. The United States was called upon to supply the Allied forces with remounts. In the four years of the war, the United States exported nearly a million horses to Europe.

The price of war
Approximately six million horses served in the First World War, and a substantial number of these were killed. When the war was over, most of the surviving horses ended up at slaughterhouses in France.

Protection
This soldier and horse both wear masks to protect them from possible gas attack.

Polish cavalry charge (above)
Thousands of Polish cavalrymen charge during training maneuvers in April 1939, a few months before the outbreak of the Second World War. While few horses were used in this war, the Polish, Russian, German, and British armies did maintain cavalry units. Horses were used mainly for logistical support.

The 61st Cavalry (below)
The Indian Army's 61st Cavalry is said to be the only remaining fully horse-mounted cavalry in the world. The Cavalry is not just for show. It participated in both the 1965 and 1971 wars with Pakistan as well as in more recent skirmishes.

THE HORSE IN SERVICE

Horses have been partners in service since 1758, when the first mounted police patrol was established in London's Bow Street. Since then, mounted divisions have become common worldwide for metropolitan police forces. In addition, horses serve on park ranger patrols, border patrols, and in military and royal ceremonial roles. These horses are often regarded as officers within their branch and as valued partners by their riders. An ideal service horse is level-headed under pressure, sturdy, sound, patient and brave—an uncommon combination of qualities. Many candidate horses do not pass training or the fitness evaluations necessary to be a service horse. But for those that do, it is the service branch that is truly rewarded.

Into the fray
Mounted police units find horses very effective for riot control because of their imposing size and their ability to put officers above the crowd. The horse's agility allows officers to respond quickly in areas where cars or motorbikes may not be able to move easily or safely.

Mounted police
Mounted police units are often pressed into service in places where a vehicle might be impractical or noisy. In tourist areas, police horses also serve as ambassadors for their police force or for their city. Here, mounted Los Angeles police patrol a city beach.

HORSE PROTECTION

Horses are not impervious to dangerous conditions when working on crowd control duties. Like modern-day gladiators, they are suited up before they go out, equipped with visors, leather nose guards, rain gear, and special boots for knee and leg protection. Police horses must go through extreme desensitization training in order to ignore stimuli that would otherwise engage their flight responses.

BORDER PATROL

Border patrol units employ horses because they can quickly—and quietly—get agents through mountainous terrain or narrow trails that are difficult to traverse by motorized transport. In addition, their size gives the agent a good vantage point from which to survey the landscape. Because of their keen sight and hearing, horses are also active partners in detecting illegal migrants and smugglers. For example, a horse's reaction to a snapping twig will alert agents to the presence of someone nearby.

Border horse
An officer with the U.S. Customs and Border Patrol Service on duty near the U S –Mexican border Sunland Park New Mexico

The Royal Service
King Juan Carlos I of Spain inspects troops and cavalry at the Palacio Real, Madrid, Spain. The Spanish Royal Guard employs about 1,500 troops, who rotate from ceremonial to active duty.

Ceremonial duties
Ceremonial horses are chosen for their size and color, as they must be similar to the others in the troop. They must also go through a temperament evaluation and rigorous training to be able to handle parades without spooking. These soldiers and their mounts are parading outside Buckingham Palace, London.

THE HORSE IN SPORT

Most equestrian sports are based around skills required of working or military horses and their riders. For example, dressage has its origins in army training, while western-style events are founded in cattle ranching. Today, riders compete from childhood to adulthood, and in most countries, male and female riders—and horses—compete on an equal playing field. The top level of equestrian sports is governed by the Fédération Equestre Internationale, which recognizes the disciplines of eventing, showjumping, dressage, endurance, vaulting, driving, and reining. Equine sporting organizations constantly strive to make sports safe for horse and rider yet, as with any athletic endeavor, injuries are inevitable. Special shoeing, feeding, equipment, and conditioning are often used to optimize performance.

Jousting (above right)
Jousting was a hugely popular spectator sport in the Middle Ages. A knight was awarded points for striking his opponent or for knocking him to the ground.

Show jumping
The athletic ability of the horse is demonstrated in show jumping, where the horse and rider navigate over fences, which sometimes include wide ditches, tall banks, and water jumps. The pair must go as fast as possible without knocking any fences down.

DRESSAGE

Classical dressage dates back to training methods used at Europe's renowned riding schools in the sixteenth and seventeenth centuries. The word "dressage" is derived from the French for "training." It developed into a sport during the twentieth century, and today is popular on every continent, particularly in Europe. Horse and rider perform a test of a certain number of compulsory movements and receive scores for each movement. As the horse progresses up the levels, tests become more complex, requiring complete harmony between horse and rider.

POLO

Speed, stamina, and agility are requisites, but bravery is the hallmark of the polo pony. Polo consists of two teams of four mounted players who try to strike a ball through the opponent's goal. Each match is divided between four and eight periods, and the team that scores the most goals wins. While it may seem like a rough sport, there is much consideration for safety of horse and rider, with penalties and fouls handed out by match officials. Polo ponies are often native stock of their country crossed with Thoroughbreds and are ponies in name only—they are actually horses. Most are mares. During the season, an average polo pony will play three games a week. Polo is played on every continent in more than 60 countries, but Argentina arguably has the best teams in the world.

Siavosh Playing Polo with Afrasiab, Persian, sixteenth century
Polo matches between nomadic warriors were first played on empty fields in China and Persia more than 2,000 years ago.

Attuned to the game (right)
The ideal polo pony intuitively knows where it is going and is highly responsive to its rider's commands. They need to be unafraid of a swinging mallet or a jostling from other horses.

Barrel racing (left)
Barrel racing, a rodeo sport dominated by women, is a timed event where the rider gallops around three barrels in a cloverleaf pattern. Most runs at the top level are performed in fewer than 18 seconds.

Roping (below)
Team roping involves a header, who attempts to rope the steer's horns, and a heeler, who ropes the hind heels. Speed and accuracy are essential for this timed event.

Buzkashi (right)
This ancient game is played in Central Asia and dates back to the days of Genghis Khan. The players must take possession of a beheaded calf or goat carcass, gallop away, and throw it into a target circle, known as the "circle of justice." Matches can last for days in traditional buzkashi, and women are not allowed to watch.

RACING

Horses are one of the fastest land animals, and this ability has been exploited over many centuries for sport. Known as "the Sport of Kings" due to its popularity with nobility beginning in the seventeenth century, today horse racing takes on several forms. Flat racing, which started with match races—two horses pitted against each other—is now the most popular form of racing found worldwide. The world's top races are the Kentucky Derby in the United States, the Epsom Derby in the United Kingdom, the Melbourne Cup in Australia, France's Prix de l'Arc de Triomphe, and the Dubai World Cup, a race with a purse of US$6 million, making it the largest purse in the world. Sprint races for Quarter Horses exist as well—this breed can sprint at 47.5 miles per hour (76.5 km/h). Other racing includes steeplechases, with horses negotiating jumps along the course, and harness racing, where the horse pulls a racing cart at the trot or pace.

Roman racing
Horse racing has been a sport of nearly every major civilization in history. This fresco from Pompeii depicts an ancient Roman chariot race.

Thoroughbred foundations
Modern racing thoroughbreds can trace their lineage back to three foundation stallions: the Godolphin Barb, the Byerly Turk, and the Darley Arabian (pictured here).

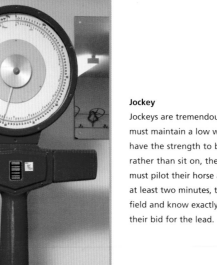

Endurance racing
Endurance racing, sanctioned by the Federation Equestre Internationale, involves riding great distances, often over difficult terrain. Awards are given for the horse that arrives first and passes all veterinary checks, as well as the horse that arrives in best condition.

Jockey
Jockeys are tremendous athletes. They must maintain a low weight yet still have the strength to balance over, rather than sit on, the horse. They must pilot their horse at full gallop for at least two minutes, through a packed field and know exactly when to make their bid for the lead.

Kentucky Derby
American flat racing culminates with the Triple Crown, where three-year-old thoroughbreds are tested under different race lengths. The Kentucky Derby, held the first Saturday in May, is the first jewel in the crown.

The Horse in Art, Literature, and Legend

Figuring prominently in both myth and people's daily lives, the horse has captured the human imagination through the ages. Some of the earliest art on record, painted on the walls of caves, feature horses, and over the centuries their appearance in painting, sculpture, and literature further illustrates the significance that horses have in human lives. Most point to the horse's outward beauty as inspiration, but there is more: an intangible spirit of freedom that exists deep under hide and mane. The horse is strength and speed, but it is also symbolic of liberty and, in a sense, vulnerability. The partnership that we have forged with a powerful yet willing, obedient creature gives inspiration to capture the horse in another way—in fable, legend, literary, and artistic endeavors.

Uffington White Horse

In an area rife with ancient stone circles, barrows, and henges lies the Uffington White Horse, an abstract hill figure, 374 feet (110 m) long, cut into a hillside in Oxfordshire, England. Recent dating suggests that the Horse is from the Bronze Age.

No one now knows the purpose of the Horse, but it most likely had religious significance. Epona, the horse goddess, was worshipped by the Celts in Gaul and had a British counterpart, Rhiannon, who dressed in glittering gold and rode a white horse.

From early depiction of horses in the Lascaux caves in France 15,000 to 20,000 years ago, to motion picture pioneer Eadweard J. Muybridge's use of a galloping horse to develop the first moving images, the horse's beauty, but more importantly its movement, has inspired artists throughout the ages. It is the horse's beauty in motion—galloping, rearing, and jumping—that makes it a challenge to capture accurately. Over time, the horse has been depicted in battle, on the hunt, and in sport. Today, the horse is still a popular subject in art, although shown mostly in the context of country or ranch life.

Whistlejacket

English painter George Stubbs (1724–1806), arguably the most famous equine artist in history, produced *Whistlejacket*, a portrait of an early Thoroughbred racehorse, around 1762. Stubbs had an extraordinary understanding of equine conformation.

Gran Cavallo

Italian artist Leonardo da Vinci (1452–1519) studied the movement and locomotion of the horse, as well as other animals. He made countless sketches of horses for the *Gran Cavallo*, an unrealized bronze sculpture.

Pegasus

In Greek mythology, Bellerophon the Valiant, son of the King of Corinth, captured Pegasus, a winged horse. Flying on Pegasus, he slew Chimera, a triple-headed monster. The legend of Pegasus has inspired artists over many centuries. Above is a painted clay fragment dated to the seventh century B.C. Below is a late-nineteenth century gold-covered bronze statue that guards the Pont Alexandre III, a bridge that spans the Seine in Paris.

Saint George

According to legend, George was a Christian soldier born in Asia Minor (modern-day Turkey) more than 1,600 years ago. It was said that Cleolinda, the daughter of the Syrian king, was to be sacrificed to a dragon that was terrorizing the town where they lived. Saint George, almost always depicted riding a white charger, kills the dragon and turns the townsfolk to Christianity. Saint George embodied bravery, chivalry, and purity, while the dragon was symbolic of evil.

Unicorn

The unicorn is not a "one-horned horse" as often believed, but rather a bearded horse/goat-like creature, with cloven hooves and a lion's tail. References to unicorns can be found in the Bible, while the ancient Greeks believed that the unicorn was an actual animal that existed in India. In Medieval religious art, unicorns were often depicted with maidens and were symbolic of chaste love and fidelity. It was thought that a unicorn could be trapped by luring them with a virgin.

31

THE BREEDS

ARABIAN

For more than 5,000 years, the Arab has been revered as the most ancient and most pure of all horse breeds—indeed, to the Arabian people, it is known as "keheilan," meaning "pure blood." To the Bedouin tribes of Arabia, the horse was not merely a conveyance; it was an instrument of war and a symbol of status—prized for its beauty, speed, and stamina. A hardy desert breed, it could survive on meager rations and its supreme turn of foot was vital in raids on rival tribes. Arguably the most beautiful of all horses, the Arab's descendants were to form the foundation of many of the world's breeds, perhaps most importantly the Thoroughbred. The Arab to this day remains unique—it has 17 ribs, 5 lumbar vertebrae and 16 tail bones; all other breeds have 18 ribs, 6 lumbar vertebrae and 18 tail bones. Its head displays the "jibbah," a shield-shaped bulge between the eyes, and its neck the "mitbah," which gives it a fine arching curve.

THE FACTS

Origin	Arabia
Color	all solid colors except palomino
Height	15.2 hands (1.57 m)
Physique	small, elegant head with dished profile, arching neck, prominent wither, sloping shoulders, short back, fine, slender legs, tail carried high
Features	fast, enduring, hardy
Temperament	brave, spirited, loyal
Use	riding, showing, competition, endurance

There is evidence of horses of fixed Arab type living on the Arabian Peninsula at least 4,500 years ago. The desert tribes of Arabia claim to trace their relationship back to a mare and a stallion that lived around 3000 B.C.

Head
Concave profile, with a shield-shaped bulge between the eyes

Eyes
Large and lustrous

Croup
Long and sloping, with tail set and carried high

Body
Compact with a short, slightly concave back

Mane and tail
Long and silky

Muzzle
Tapered to a small end

Neck
Arched, long, with head held high

The Arab is a desert breed, able to survive in dry, extremely hot conditions.

Legs
Long and slender, tendons clearly defined

Feet
Small and hard

The Arab stallion Imperial Shehaab. The Bedouin favored lighter-colored horses as they could better withstand the heat of the desert sun.

THOROUGHBRED

Three stallions were to form the foundation of the mighty Thoroughbred, the equine powerhouse that launched the Sport of Kings. These stallions—the Godolphin Arabian, the Darley Arabian, and the Byerley Turk—can today be found in the lineage of 93 percent of all modern Thoroughbreds. The Godolphin Arabian was originally used as a teaser—to test if a mare is in season before being put to the real "star"—and is said to have fought another horse for a mare. The Darley Arabian was found in Syria in 1704 and was the great-great-grandsire of Eclipse, perhaps the most famous racehorse of all time. The Byerley Turk, despite his name, is likely to have been a Barb or Akhal-Teke. He was to found the line from which came Diomed, winner of the first Epsom Derby in 1780.

ANCESTRY

The Thoroughbred breed was formed from Arab stallions put to native running stock, to give it more speed.

Native running horses
Irish Hobby
Barb
Scottish Galloway
Arab
Thoroughbred

A beautiful Thoroughbred enjoys its freedom with an explosive burst of speed at Whiskey Creek Farm, Virginia, U.S.A.

THE FACTS	
Origin	England
Color	all solid colors except palomino
Height	16 hands (1.63 m)
Physique	refined head, lean neck, sloping shoulder, prominent wither, long back, powerful quarters, long, slender legs
Features	noble, swift, elegant
Temperament	spirited, intelligent
Use	racing, competition

The Thoroughbred originated in early eighteenth-century England. It was soon exported to the American Colonies and, later, mainland Europe. For centuries, Thoroughbred breeding in England has been centered around the town of Newmarket in Suffolk.

Head
Refined and elegant, straight profile

Quarters
Strong and powerful, tail medium set

Back
Long in proportion

Neck
Arched and well-muscled

Shoulders
Long and well-sloped, from prominent wither

Legs
Long and slender, with well-formed joints, good bone, and powerful hocks

Feet
Well-made and in proportion, very sound

The Thoroughbred is not just renowned for its speed; it also makes a superlative competition horse.

PRZEWALSKI'S HORSE

Sometimes known as the Asiatic Wild Horse, Przewalski's Horse provides a valuable link between the earliest equines and today's modern horse. It is named for Colonel Nicolai Mikhailovitch Przewalski, who discovered wild herds of this distinctive animal in the Tachin Schah—Mountains of the Yellow Horse—on the edge of the Gobi desert in 1879. Cave paintings dating back some 20,000 years found across parts of Europe depict a horse very similar to the Przewalski's Horse. It features very frequently in these paintings, suggesting it was found in abundance. The Przewalski Horse is unique in that it has 66 chromosomes—all other breeds have 64. Bred to a domestic horse, it will produce fertile offspring that have 65 chromosomes. Efforts have been made in recent years to reintroduce the Przewalski's Horse back into the wild, notably in the Ukraine, the Netherlands, China, and Mongolia, its original home.

THE FACTS	
Origin	Mongolia
Color	yellow-dun, black points
Height	13 hands (1.32 m)
Physique	long, plain head, thickset neck, no discernible wither, upright shoulder, straight back
Temperament	fierce and aggressive in the wild
Use	wild horse

About 20,000 years ago, Przewalski's Horse roamed over vast areas of Europe and Central Asia. When Nicolai Przewalski discovered the breed in 1879, they were restricted to present-day Mongolia, mostly around the western edges of the Gobi desert.

Head
Large and rather heavy, convex profile, sometimes with a "mealy" muzzle

Mane and tail
Black, upright mane, short hairs at the top of the tail

Back
Straight, very little wither, a dorsal stripe and sometimes a cross over the wither

Color
"Primitive" coloring of yellowish-dun, with black points

Neck
Thickset and straight

Przewalski's Horses at home in the Gobi desert, China. This is one of the harshest environments on Earth—water is scarce and there are huge extremes of heat and cold.

Legs
Zebra-striped

Przewalski's Horses in the Endangered Species Research Center of Gansu Province, China, shortly before being released into the wild

ALTAI

For many centuries the tribesmen of the Altai Mountains in southern Siberia depended utterly on their horses to maintain their nomadic way of life in a wild and unforgiving part of the world. Mountain trails cut into rock, criss-crossed with rapid streams and rivers, were not easy to cross, so the Altai needed to be both surefooted and agile. Little is known about the ancestry of this enigmatic breed. The Altai often has the extravagantly spotted coat seen in the Appaloosa, but is thought to be of ancient origin; its dished face is reminiscent of the Arab, although there is nothing to suggest Oriental influence. The modern Altai is prized as an outcross—mixed with, for example, the Russian Heavy Draft breed, it produced a sizeable animal of considerable power and strength.

THE FACTS	
Origin	Central Asia
Color	chestnut, black, bay, gray, spotted
Height	13.3 hands (1.40 m)
Physique	large head with dished profile, short, rather fleshy neck; dipped back, deep chest, muscular croup, strong, hard legs and feet
Features	enduring, hardy
Temperament	biddable, docile
Use	pack, harness, trek

The Altai Mountain range covers a vast region spanning four countries: Russia, Kazakhstan, China, and Mongolia. The Altai had to be hardy to survive the bitterly cold winters.

Head
Large and rather coarse, sometimes slightly concave in profile

Quarters
Muscular and well-formed

Back
Long and with a tendency to be dipped

Neck
Short and fleshy

Chest
Plenty of heart room

Legs
Well set-on but quite short

Feet
Hard, dark horn

Kazak horsemen galloping across the frozen steppes of central Asia. They traditionally hunt on horseback with the aid of trained golden eagles.

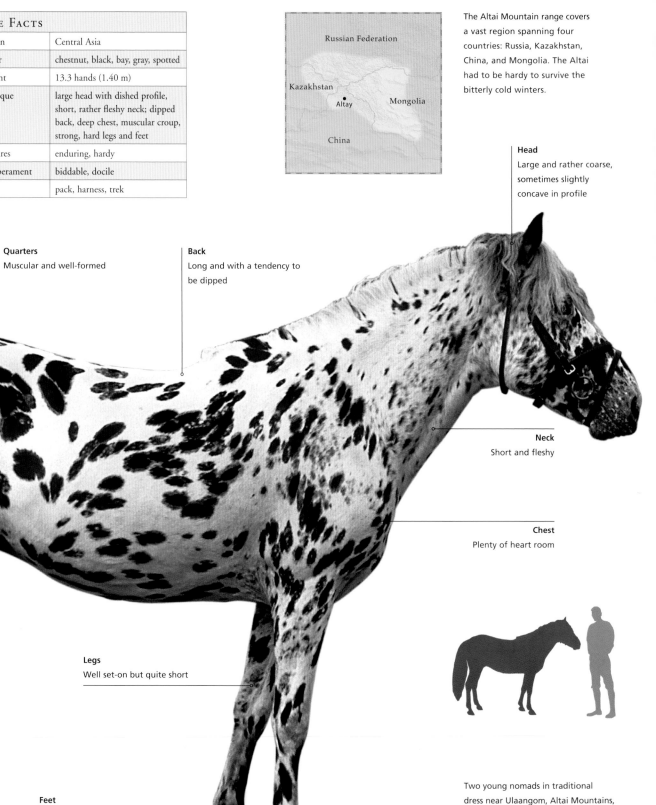

Two young nomads in traditional dress near Ulaangom, Altai Mountains, western Mongolia

CAMARGUE

Where the Rhône meets the Mediterranean there is a land of marsh, lake, and pasture known as the Camargue. Dotted across this landscape are ghostly white shapes of the region's indigenous horses. These enchanting animals are thought to be among the few modern breeds that are completely free of Arab blood. They are possibly related to the ancient, and now extinct, Solutré Horse. They are known as "the horses of the sea," and their environment is harsh: fearsome heat during the summer, icy cold in winter months, and ravaged by the salt-laden mistral wind that blows across their marshland home. Camargue Horses are used by the wetlands cowboys, known as gardians, to round up the tough little black bulls of the region, which are destined for the bullfighting rings of southern France. The horses are now a protected breed, rounded up each year to be branded—colts or stallions deemed unsuitable for breeding are gelded.

THE FACTS	
Origin	southeast France
Color	always gray
Height	14 hands (1.42 m)
Physique	rather coarse, plain head, short neck, upright shoulder, deep chest, compact body, short, well-formed legs
Features	rugged, tough, easy keeper
Temperament	lively, intelligent, spirited
Use	herding, riding, endurance riding

The Camargue is Western Europe's largest river delta and a place of great ecological significance. It was designated as a nature reserve in 1927 and granted National Park status in 1970.

Head
Tends to be rather heavy and coarse

Body
Generally compact, with a short, strong back

Neck
Short and muscular

Shoulders
Upright, leading to a short, choppy stride

Quarters
Sloping with a short croup

The famous "white horses of the sea" at the Camargue Festival held each May in the town of Port-Saint-Louis-du-Rhône.

Legs
Short and well-made, with good joints

Feet
Very hard and sound, rarely need shoeing

The horses of the Camargue have adapted supremely to their home of marsh and sea. They survive on scrub, reeds, tough grass, and saltwort, a flowering plant that is tolerant of salt.

CASPIAN

An American traveler named Louise Firouz discovered herds of tiny horses on the edge of the Caspian Sea in 1965. But these little horses—rather like an Arab in miniature—are thought to be of great antiquity. Some authorities say that Caspian is the oldest horse breed still extant, apart from Przewalkski's Horse. Small horses of considerable quality are depicted in reliefs and other artifacts from ancient Egypt and on the famous seal of the Persian king, Darius the Great (c. 522–486 B.C.). The seal shows Darius in a chariot drawn by two horses, slaying a much larger lion. The Caspian has several unique features, including a "vaulted head," caused by an unusual formation of the bones of the forehead; a shoulder blade that is wider at the base than at the top; and an extra molar in the lower jaw. Despite its stature— the Caspian rarely exceeds 12 hands (1.22 m) in height—it is considered a small horse, not a pony.

THE FACTS	
Origin	northern Iran
Color	bay, gray, chestnut, black
Height	12 hands (1.22 m)
Physique	small, quality head, elegant, supple neck, short-coupled, well-developed quarters, slender legs, hard feet
Features	fleet of foot, agile, strong
Temperament	gentle, affectionate, biddable
Use	riding, show, harness

The Caspian breed was discovered by Louise Firouz in villages around Amol, on the shores of the Caspian Sea in northern Iran.

Head
Tapered muzzle, slightly concave face, vaulted forehead

Back
Slim and narrow, but with depth through the girth

Neck
Long and supple

Quarters
Powerful and well-muscled

Shoulders
Nicely sloping to give a long, low stride, prominent wither

A Caspian in an English field. The breed is rare, but no longer in danger of extinction thanks to the efforts of breeders in Iran, England, and the United States.

Legs
Long and slender, with plenty of dense, flat bone

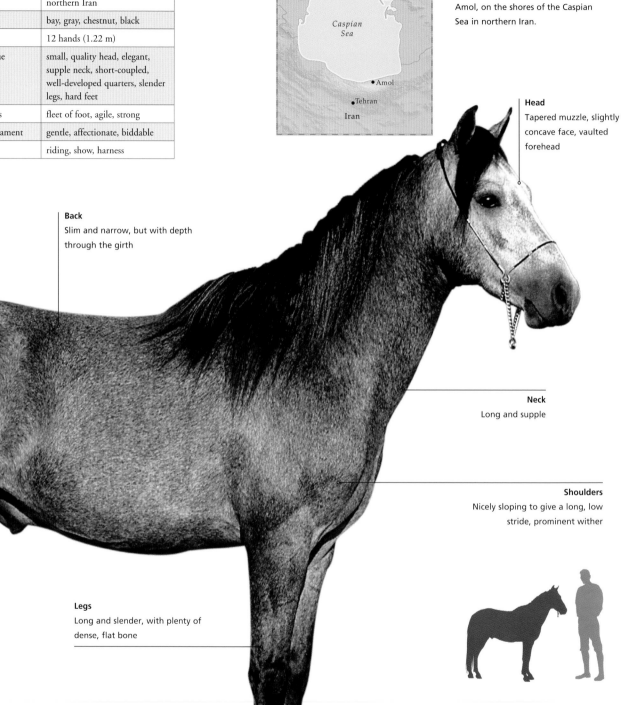

Caspian Horses pictured in Iran—the unique vaulted forehead of the breed can clearly be seen on the gray and on the foal.

Feet
Oval in shape and exceptionally hard

HUCUL

This ancient breed, indigenous to the Carpathian Mountains, takes its name from the Huculsko region in what is now Romania. The invading Mongols are thought to have introduced the breed to the region in the Middle Ages. Sometimes called the Carpathian Pony, the Hucul roots undoubtedly lie in the Tarpan, perhaps the results of outcrossings to the Mongolian Pony. The first mention of an equine similar to the Hucul was some 400 years ago, when it was referred to as the "Mountain Tarpan," further evidence of its connection to the primitive horse. The primitive dun coloring with black points and zebra striping is sometimes seen in the Hucul. Because of the isolation of its mountainous home, it has rarely been cross-bred, keeping the breed remarkably pure. Today, the Hucul is valued highly as a pack animal, strong enough to carry a heavy load, and surefooted enough to traverse the steep mountain trails of its homeland.

THE FACTS	
Origin	Carpathian Mountains, Eastern Europe
Color	predominantly dun with black points, bay, brown, gray
Height	13 hands (1.32 m)
Physique	short, blunt head, short neck, flat withers, upright shoulders, compact body, short legs, sound feet
Features	surefooted, hardy, sturdy
Temperament	docile, gentle, easy going
Use	pack, forestry, trekking

The Carpathian Mountains span Romania, Ukraine, Slovakia, and Poland. The first Hucul stud farm was established at Radauti in Romania in 1856 using the foundation stallions Goral, Hroby, Ousor, Pietrousu, and Prislop.

Head
Short, rather blunt, but not unattractive

Back
Compact and strong, proportionate

Neck
Short and well-muscled, pronounced wither

Shoulders
Slightly sloping, giving the animal freedom of movement

Tail
Set and carried high, thick coarse hair

The Hucul is sometimes referred to as the "Mountain Tarpan" and its similarities to the ancient horse are clear.

Legs
Very hard and strong, dense bone

Feet
Tough and sound

Right, clockwise from top center: A Hucul woman in traditional dress stands beside her horse, which carries slender barrels of milk. Jasina, Ukraine, c. 1920.

Two horses in a traditional harness in Ukraine.

Huculs grazing on steppe grassland in the Aggtelek National Park, Hungary.

KONIK

Like the Hucul, the Polish Konik is thought to be closely related to the extinct Tarpan. It, too, is diminutive in stature—its name translates as "little horse"—but it has few pony qualities. It is widespread throughout Poland and is valued as an agricultural animal in rural areas. It is extremely strong for its height, which is rarely higher than 13 hands (1.32 m), and is of heavier build—more of a draft animal—than the Hucul. Some Arabian blood has been added to the breed in recent years, to give it more refined qualities, which has also introduced coloring other than its original variations of the primitive dun. In 1933, two German scientists crossed the breed with Przewalski's Horse and Icelandic blood to try to re-establish a Tarpan herd. Other breeding programs have created horses with Tarpan characteristics but it is hard to see what benefits these experiments would have to the equine world as a whole.

THE FACTS	
Origin	Poland
Color	predominantly dun with black points
Height	13 hands (1.32 m)
Physique	large head, muscular neck, low wither, upright shoulder, broad body, good legs
Features	hardy, easy keeper, strong
Temperament	calm, docile, biddable
Use	agriculture, harness, riding

Once bred throughout Poland by farmers, today the Konik is mainly bred at the state stud at Popielno. Semi-wild herds are preserved in the Bialowieza Forest in the east of Poland.

Head
Large but in proportion to the overall frame, rather coarse

Back
Broad and strong, deep through the girth

Neck
Short and powerful

Quarters
Wide and muscular, tail set quite low

Shoulders
Upright, with flat wither, making the Konik well-suited to harness

The Konik's large head is a feature shared with extinct wild breeds of Europe and Asia.

Legs and feet
Well-made and hardy

The ancient markings of the Tarpan—the distinctive eel or dorsal stripes along the spine and the gray-dun, or grullo, coloring—are clearly seen in this herd of Koniks.

ARIEGEOIS

Julius Caesar described a mountain breed of horse in his *Commentaries on the Gallic War* and all evidence suggests that he was describing the Ariègeois, a heavy draft type that takes its name from the Ariège River in the French Pyrenees. It is one of three pony breeds considered native to France, the others being the Landais and the Pottok. Cave paintings found near the village of Niaux depict a small, heavy equine that recalls both the Camargue and the Ariègeois. The breed is similar to the Dales and Fell ponies of northern England in that it is always black, with few or no white markings, which suggests a genetic connection with the Friesian of the Netherlands. The Ariègeois is a stocky, robust little horse whose size is belied by its strength and endurance. Its uses have changed over the years, but it was almost certainly used for smuggling across the French–Spanish border, where its stamina and stoic patience would have been a boon.

THE FACTS	
Origin	France and Spain
Color	black, few or no white markings
Height	14.3 hands (1.50 m)
Physique	small, refined head, short, strong neck, long back, rounded quarters, hard feet
Features	easy keeper, robust, hardy
Temperament	docile, quiet
Use	pack, agriculture, harness

Occasionally referred as the Merens Pony, from one of the villages in the region, the Ariègeois is named for the Ariège River. It is a mountain type that owes its extreme hardiness to its harsh environment.

Head
Refined and pretty, with wide-set eyes

Coat
Always black, with burnished reddish brown highlights in winter months

Back
Rather long, typical in a pack type of equine

Neck
Short and muscular, well set-on

Quarters
Muscular and sloping, tail set low

Shoulders
Gently sloping, well-made

Chest
Powerful and deep

An Ariègeois, with friend, in the Spanish Pyrenees

Legs
Short, a tendency towards cowhocks

Feet
Well-made and very sound, some feather

The sturdy and sensible Ariègeois makes a superb harness animal—although small, it is immensely strong.

LANDAIS

The Landais originated on the plains and marshes of the Landes region in southwestern France. It is sometimes known as the Barthais, which was once a separate breed that originated from the marshlands around the Adour River. It is not known when the two breeds merged. This ancient breed, thought to be related to the extinct Tarpan, was undoubtedly influenced by Arab blood following the Battle of Tours and Poitiers in A.D. 732 when the French held off a Muslim invasion. Further Arabian blood was introduced in 1913 to increase size and add refinement. Today's Landais resembles a miniature Arab, albeit a more sturdy one. At the beginning of the twentieth century, there were an estimated 2,000 Landais running wild. The breed suffered a severe decline after the Second World War but efforts have since been made to restabilize it, with a studbook being opened in 1975.

THE FACTS	
Origin	southwest France
Color	bay, brown, chestnut, black
Height	13.1 hands (1.35 m)
Physique	neat, pretty head with plenty of space between the eyes, supple neck, pronounced wither, sloping shoulder, straight back, sloping quarters, high-set tail
Features	elegant, robust
Temperament	trainable, but can be willful
Use	riding, harness

The Landes region of southwestern France includes extensive marshlands, Europe's longest beach, Cote D'Argent, and Europe's biggest pine forest. Ponies are thought to have lived in the region for at least 2,000 years.

Bay of Biscay

•Bordeaux

France

Spain

Head
Refined and neat, of Arab character

Back
Short and compact

Wither
Prominent

Neck
Muscular and supple

Shoulders
Nicely sloping, probably due to the recent Arab influence

Quarters
Well-muscled and sloping, tail set and carried high

A Landais pictured at the National Stud at Pau, on the northern edge of the French Pyrenees.

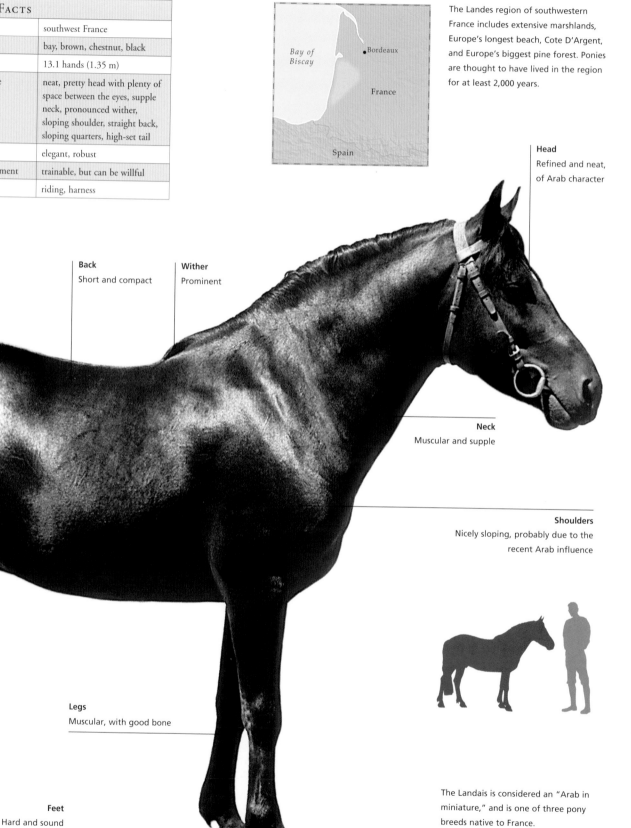

Legs
Muscular, with good bone

Feet
Hard and sound

The Landais is considered an "Arab in miniature," and is one of three pony breeds native to France.

52

POTTOK

France's third native breed of pony originates from the Basque region, where it proved invaluable as a pack animal in the mountains along the French–Spanish border. It is an ancient breed, thought to have its roots in the now-extinct Magdalenian horses of 14,000–7,000 B.C. Once roaming wild, the Pottok is now domesticated, and, over the centuries, has been used both in the mining industry and, more romantically, by smugglers. The pure Pottok suffered from outcrossing in the twentieth century, when stockier animals were in demand for agriculture and broken-coated examples—piebald and skewbald— were popular in circuses. At one time, there were fewer than 150 breeding pure Pottok mares left. There are now two sections of the studbook, opened in 1970: studbook A for pure-breds, and B for cross-breds, usually with Arabs or Welsh Section B.

THE FACTS	
Origin	Basque region, France
Color	all colors
Height	14 hands (1.42 m)
Physique	straight head, sometimes with a little dishing, small ears, short neck, straight shoulders, long back, good legs, hard feet
Features	sturdy, enduring, easy feeder
Temperament	calm, docile, gentle
Use	riding, harness, all-rounder

A reserve in Bidarray, Basse-Navarre, has been established to save the breed from extinction. There are annual Pottok fairs in Espelette each November and January.

Head
Generally attractive, sometimes lightly dished, small ears

Back
Long but generally well-formed

Neck
Rather short in proportion

Some of the studbook A Pottoks are allowed to roam free in the Basque mountains and are rounded-up annually.

Shoulders
Straight, rather than sloping

Legs
Fine and lean, clean joints

Feet
Small and round, extremely hard

Broken-coated Pottok ponies were once in demand for use in circuses—the coloring was the result of outcrossings, not all of them successful.

NORIKER

This breed's name comes from Noricum, a province of the Roman Empire that now comprises modern Austria—an indication of the antiquity of this breed. With the network of roads for which the Romans are renowned, a superior pack and draft horse was required, and the Noriker is probably based on the heavy draft horses of the period. From about 1565, the monasteries, which have played such a part in conserving and preserving the world's horse breeds, took control of breeding the compact, surefooted little horses and the Noriker type was fixed and documented. Strict guidelines for breeding were introduced in the seventeenth century, with regulations for the first stallion inspections drawn up in 1703. The breed suffered mixed fortunes, as demand for lighter, more elegant riding types grew and outcrosses were introduced. But the modern Noriker remains a sturdy, good-looking little horse, with quality as well as strength.

THE FACTS	
Origin	Austria
Color	black, bay, chestnut, roan, spotted
Height	15 hands (1.52 m)
Physique	large head, straight or convex profile, crested neck, good shoulders with some slope, broad body, deep girth, strong quarters, powerful legs, good feet
Features	strong, surefooted, robust
Temperament	quiet, biddable
Use	harness, riding, pack, forestry

The Noriker is native to the mountainous region of southern Austria. Since ancient times breeding efforts have been concentrated around Salzburg.

Head
Rather heavy, straight or convex profile

Quarters
Rounded and muscular, often with a broad cleft, low-set tail

Body
In proportion, well-sprung ribs

Neck
Short and thickset

Shoulders
Have a tendency to be loaded, but this does not affect the stride

Chest
Deep and well-formed

Legs
Well-made and strong, some feather

Feet
Hard and sound

A team of six spotted Norikers pull a carriage through the town of Rottach-Egern, southern Bavaria, Germany.

Right, clockwise from top left:
A striking Noriker, whose coloring stands out against the snow.

The quiet and biddable Noriker makes an excellent harness horse.

The Noriker is named for the ancient Noricum, and remains a sturdy, sensible, and good-looking little horse.

PINDOS

Developed from an ancient Greek breed in the region of
Thessaly, the Pindos is sometimes called the Thessalian
Pony, although the modern horse is unlikely to bear much
resemblance to its ancient forebears. In the third century A.D.,
the Greek poet Oppian described the Thessalian horse as
"most noted for beauty, courage, and endurance," although only
the latter two descriptors could be said to apply to the Pindos.
Its original homeland was far from conducive to horse breeding.
Infertile soil, poor vegetation, and extremes of weather produced
a frugal and robust creature—qualities that made up for its
conspicuous lack of beauty. The region is mountainous, so the Pindos
is a surefooted and confident climber. Since ancient times, it has
absorbed other since-forgotten breeds, such as the Peloponnese,
Arcadian, and Epidaurian. The modern Pindos is an
easy-keeping all-rounder, still of value to the
peoples of Thessaly.

The Facts	
Origin	Greece
Color	black, bay, gray, roan
Height	13 hands (1.32 m)
Physique	plain head with small eyes, narrow neck, pronounced wither, long back, weak quarters, slender legs, hard feet
Features	frugal, agile, surefooted
Temperament	biddable, willing but can be stubborn
Use	pack, harness, riding, agriculture

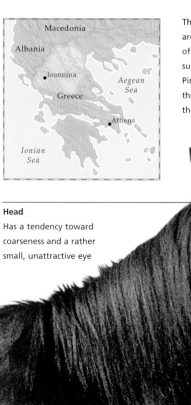

The traditional horse-breeding
areas of Greece were the lowlands
of Thessaly and Epirus, which are
surrounded by the mountains of
Pindos, Othrys, Ossa, and Agrafa,
through which flows the Pineios River
that drains into the Aegean Sea.

Head
Has a tendency toward
coarseness and a rather
small, unattractive eye

Back
Long and narrow

Withers
Pronounced

Neck
Narrow, lacking in muscle

Quarters
Weak and underdeveloped, tail is set high,
which suggests some Oriental influence

Shoulders
Nicely sloping, probably due to
recent Arab influence

A shepherd in the Pindos mountain
range with his reliable pony

Legs
Slender and lacking bone, poor
conformation

The Pindos' natural home was
harsh and has produced a tough
and enduring horse. What the
modern Pindos lacks in good looks,
it more than makes up for with
its good-natured robustness.

Feet
Boxy and small, but very hard

AKHAL-TEKE

Alexander the Great, Marco Polo, and Gengis Khan are said to have been fans of this golden equine aristocrat, which is thought to be as ancient as the Arab, if not older. It is a desert breed, like the Arab, and originates from the Karakum Desert in Turkmenistan, a harsh, unforgiving environment. It takes its name from a Turkmen tribe called the Teke, who lived in the Akhal region. The tribesmen held their horses in high regard, feeding them on a mix of grains and animal fats when fresh grass was scarce, and blanketing them against the fierce cold. The Russians annexed Turkmenistan in the 1880s and called its horses "Argamaks," which translates as "tall and refined." The first official Akhal-Teke stud, Zakaspiisky, was founded using the best stock, including the stallion Boinou, forebear of some of the breeding lines used today.

THE FACTS	
Origin	Turkmenistan
Color	chestnut, bay, gray, palomino (isabella), dun and black
Height	15.1 hands (1.55 m)
Physique	fine, thin head, lean, high-set neck, sloping shoulder, long back, clean legs
Features	elegant, athletic, hardy
Temperament	intelligent, calm
Use	riding, competition, endurance

The Akhal-Teke originated in the Akhal region where the Kopet Dag mountain range meets the Karakum Desert. The environment was harsh, and the breed had to be able to tolerate extreme heat, dry cold, and drought.

The Akhal-Teke is considered a national treasure in Turkmenistan and there are strict controls on exports.

Mane and tail
Rather thin and sparse

Back
Rather long, muscular croup

Coat
Distinctive metallic sheen

Neck
Long and upright, set on high wither

Shoulders
Sloping, well-muscled

Legs
Fine and hard, although lacking in the sport horse's well-defined second thigh

Feet
Hard and sound

Two Akhal-Tekes in ornate traditional bridles prior to racing at the hippodrome in Ashgabat, capital of Turkmenistan.

ANGLO ARAB

If the aim is to produce a horse with speed and strength as well as endurance and beauty, the crossing of the Arab with the Thoroughbred is almost too obvious. The Anglo Arab was first created not, as its name suggests, in England, but in Germany in 1892. But it was the French who perpetuated the breed. In the mid-nineteenth century, a French expert named Eugène Guyot experimented with breeding the progeny of a Thoroughbred–Arab back to a Thoroughbred, then the offspring of that union back to the Arab. The favored mix is no more than 75 percent Arab blood and no less than 25 percent. The resulting horse is tough, trainable, and good-looking. It is taller than the Arab and of slightly heavier build than the Thoroughbred, but it has great speed and athleticism and makes a superlative competition horse. It excels in the show ring, in show jumping, and in the dressage arena.

THE FACTS	
Origin	Germany
Color	all solid colors
Height	16.2 hands (1.68 m)
Physique	attractive head with straight profile, long neck, fine shoulders, long, slender legs
Features	intelligent, willing
Temperament	intelligent, calm
Use	competition, riding

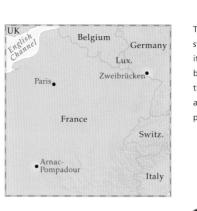

The Anglo Arab was first created at a stud farm Zweibrucken in Germany but it was the French who perpetuated the breed at Pompadour in the south of the Limousin region. Its success as an all-round performance horse makes it popular worldwide.

An Anglo Arab mare and her foal, pictured in Sardinia—the breed's appeal is worldwide.

Neck
Muscular and well-set, with prominent wither

Body
Compact and strong

Head
The Thoroughbred influence is apparent in the Anglo Arab's straight profile

Shoulders
Sloping to guarantee good action

Legs
Long and fine, good joints and clean bone

Feet
Exceptionally strong and sound

France's Eric Vigeanel rides the Anglo Arab Coronado Prior in the cross-country phase of the three-day event at the Beijing Olympic Games 2008.

Alex Hua Tian makes history as China's first ever competitor in the Olympic three-day event at Beijing 2008 on the Anglo Arab Chico.

SHAGYA ARAB

Developed 200 years ago as a military horse, the Shagya Arab is slightly taller and less finely built than the Arab, although it has all its temperament and quality. It takes its name from the founding sire of the breed, the stallion Shagya, which was unusually tall for an Arab, standing at around 15.2 hands, and a distinctive cream color. Shagya was bought for the Hungarian National Stud at Babolna, where he stood from 1836 to 1842, passing his good looks and athleticism to his offspring—most importantly, to several sons, who continued the line. The breed served its purpose well as a swift, enduring, and hardy cavalry mount, but today it is popular as a riding and competition horse. It also makes a good carriage horse.

THE FACTS	
Origin	Hungary
Color	predominantly gray
Height	16 hands (1.63 m)
Physique	fine, attractive head, elegant neck, sloping shoulder, medium-length back, excellent legs
Features	elegant, athletic, handsome
Temperament	willing, brave, friendly
Use	riding, competition

Shagya, the founding sire, was bred by the Bani Saher bedouin tribe in what was then Syria and came to Babolna in 1836. As well as in Hungary, it is now bred in Germany, Poland, Austria, the Czech Republic, Slovakia, and Russia.

Head
The Arab influence is clear in the fine, elegant head, which is often slightly concave in profile

Body
Compact and strong, more substantial than the pure-bred Arab while still being Arabian in appearance

Neck
Elegant and fine, slightly arched

ANCESTRY

The Shagya combines all the good looks, elegance, endurance, and speed of the pure-bred Arab with the requirements of the modern riding horse.

Arab
English Thoroughbred
Lipizzaner
Shagya Arab

The Shagya Arab was originally bred as a military mount, and is swift and enduring.

Legs
Strong and clean, good bone

Feet
Hard and dry, typical of a desert-type breed

Most Shagya Arabs are gray, perhaps a throwback to the breed's eponymous foundation sire, which was a distinctive pale cream color.

BARB

There is a school of thought that the Barb, which originated in North Africa, shares a common ancestor with the Arab, which is indicative in several features. The Akhal-Teke also shows similarities. Some believe that one of the three foundation sires of the English Thoroughbred, the Godolphin Arabian, was actually a Barb. The breed's antiquity is in no doubt. It was prized by the Berbers of North Africa for its lightning speed and durability, which made it an exceptional warhorse. The Barb stands slightly taller than the Arab and, like its eastern counterpart, has played a significant role in the evolution of the world's breeds. Its straight and noble head can be seen in both the Andalusian and Lusitano, and its influence is evident in the white horses of the Camargue and the wild American Mustang.

The Barb originated in North Africa and, like the Arab and the Akhal-Teke, is a desert type.

THE FACTS	
Origin	North Africa
Color	bay, black, gray, chestnut
Height	15.2 hands (1.57 m)
Physique	long, fine head with convex or straight profile, upright shoulder, strong back, deep girth, neat, narrow feet
Features	fast, hardy, durable
Temperament	fiery, uncertain temper, intelligent
Use	riding horse, breeding outcross

The Barb originated in Maghreb region of northwest Africa, but horses of similar type were also found in Morocco, Algeria, and Tunisia, where varying types of Barb still exist. Barb Horses were introduced to Spain during the Moorish invasions and influenced the Andalusian and Lusitano.

Head
Straight profile, occasionally slightly convex

Neck
Arched, well-set with often prominent wither

Croup
Narrow and sloping, with low-set tail

Shoulders
Well-muscled but sometimes rather upright

Legs
Front legs can sometimes be set close; hind limbs can be cow-hocked

Feet
Small and rather boxy, but tough and sound

While it has had enormous influence on the world's breeds, it is now rare to find a pure-bred Barb, although a strain called the Spanish Barb (opposite page) is popular in America.

KARABAKH

A mountain-steppe breed, the Karabakh takes its name from the region of Azerbaijan where it originated. It shares similarities with both the Arab and the Akhal-Teke. Certainly, it has the iridescent sheen of the latter, and the small head and elegant conformation of the former. Some historical sources record a successful Arab invasion of Azerbaijan in the eighth to ninth century, when tens of thousands of golden chestnut horses—the predominant color of the Karabakh—were taken by the conquerors. So it is possible that the Karabakh have played a role in the development of the Arab. The Karabakh ruler, Ibrahim-Khalil Khan (1730–1806), is believed to have possessed a herd of Karabakhs numbering 3,000 to 4,000. It was later to become a popular breed in Europe. Latterly, the Karabakh has influenced other breeds, notably the Russian Don.

THE FACTS	
Origin	Azerbaijan
Color	chestnut, bay, dun
Height	15 hands (1.52 m)
Physique	small head with wide forehead, elegant neck, compact, narrow body, long, elegant legs
Features	agile, athletic, tough
Temperament	calm, willing, brave
Use	racing, riding, harness

The Karabakh takes its name from the region of Nagorny Karabakh in Azerbaijan between the Aras and Kura rivers. Breed numbers are small, but efforts are being made to regenerate it.

Neck
Medium length, elegant but strong, set on average height wither

Coat
A distinctive golden glow like that of the Akhal-Teke

Body
Compact and powerful, with muscular quarters and low-set tail

The Karabakh has the fine, sculpted head of the Arab, but without the pronounced "dishing" in profile.

Head
Small and straight, alert expression

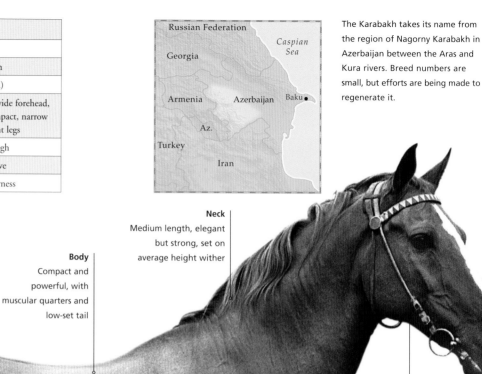

Legs
Long and slender, with small joints

Right, clockwise from left:
The Karabakh is a favored mount of herdsmen in the Caucasus Mountains.

A herd of Karabakhs grazing in the rugged mountains for which they are superbly adapted.

The Karabakh is fast, agile, and sure-footed.

AVELIGNESE

Italy's version of the Haflinger stands taller than its Austrian counterpart, although the two are thought to share a common ancestor in 133 El Bedavi XXII, an oriental stallion bought to Austria from Arabia. Certainly, there is a striking resemblance between the two, with the chunkier Avelignese sharing the Haflinger's striking color. The Avelignese is widely bred throughout Tuscany, Emilia, and central southern Italy and is considered to be the most prolific Italian breed. Although it certainly has oriental blood back through El Bedavi, it is considered to be a coldblooded breed and has several coldblood traits, not least its placid and amenable temperament. Robust and hardy, the Avelignese is the perfect family pony—stocky enough to carry an adult, and kind and gentle enough to look after the smallest child.

THE FACTS	
Origin	Italy
Color	golden chestnut with flaxen mane and tail
Height	14.3 hands (1.50 m)
Physique	small head, crested neck, strong shoulders, deep, muscular chest, wide back, good feet
Features	sturdy, surefooted, attractive
Temperament	placid, robust, unflappable
Use	harness, trekking, pack

The Avelignese takes its name from Avalengo, an area of the Trentino Alto Adige in northern Italy, on the border with Austria. It is closely related to the Austrian Haflinger

Head
Small and pretty, rather pony-like

Back
Substantial and broad, with strong, well-muscled quarters

Neck
Muscular and crested, leading to strong but sometimes upright shoulders

The Avelignese is always chestnut with an abundant flaxen mane and tail.

Chest
Wide and deep, with plenty of heart room

Legs
Generally good, with plenty of hard bone and well-formed joints, occasionally some feather

An Avelignese at the Instituto Ippico—the Institute of the Horse—in Crema, Italy.

Feet
Exceptionally strong and sound

HAFLINGER

This breed originated high in the southern Tyrolean Mountains in present day Austria and Italy; where its innate surefootedness was invaluable to farmers on the rocky alpine slopes. All modern pure-bred Haflingers must be able to trace their ancestry back to one stallion—249 Folie sired by the part-bred Arab 133 El Bedavi XXII and out of a native Tyrolean mare. Although military demands during the Second World War resulted in a more sturdy, draft type of horse, breeders since have placed the emphasis back on elegance. Today's Haflinger is a small but tough, athletic horse, with striking coloring and noble good looks. The Austrian Haflingers bear the famous Edelweiss brand mark—a flower with an "H" in the center—and they are often referred to as Edelweiss Ponies.

THE FACTS	
Origin	Austria
Color	all ranges of chestnut from palest gold to deep liver, white or flaxen mane and tail
Height	13.3 hands (1.40 m)
Physique	neat, pretty head, well-made shoulders, deep girth, long back, excellent legs and feet
Features	hardy, strong, athletic
Temperament	gentle, kind, amenable
Use	riding, harness, pack, forestry

The Haflinger takes its name from the village of Hafling, which until 1918 was within the borders of Austria. It was originally used for crossing steep mountain passes and as a light agricultural horse.

Head
Lean and refined, with large, expressive eyes

Mane and tail
White or flaxen, fairly abundant

Coat
Varies from the palest gold to rich vibrant chestnut

Neck
Medium length, with pronounced wither

Shoulders
Well-made, sloping shoulders

The Haflinger stallion Milan—the breed is athletic and spirited.

Legs
Clean and strong, with plenty of bone, and good feet

Right, clockwise from top: Haflingers Shane and Murphy at a Texas farm. The first Haflingers were imported into the United States in the 1950s.

A herd of galloping Haflingers.

The Haflinger has a very pretty, pony-type head.

TERSK

Originally named Streletsky, for the stud on which the breed was founded, the Tersk or Tersky was developed in the nineteenth century as a military mount. Arab and Anglo Arab stallions were used on Karabakh, Orlov, Persian, and Turkmenian mares, and the resulting breed was everything the cavalry required—willing, gentle, intelligent, and most of all fleet of foot. Although by the 1920s the Streletsky horses had been virtually wiped out in the turmoil of war, two stallions remained, Tsenitel and Tsilindr, both by the influential sire Tsenny. A handful of surviving mares were also located, and Don, Kabardin, and Arab blood was introduced. The breeding program began in 1925 at the Tersk Stud, for which the new breed was named.

THE FACTS

Origin	Ukraine
Color	predominantly gray
Height	15.1 hands (1.55 m)
Physique	straight head, elegant neck, deep chest, muscular quarters, good, hard legs, high-set tail
Features	sound, enduring, hardy
Temperament	kind, willing, intelligent
Use	racing, endurance, competition

The breed was originally known as the Streletsky, for the Ukrainian stud on which it was founded. Almost wiped out during the years of civil war, it was re-established at the Tersk Stud, near the Caucasus Mountains.

ANCESTRY

Similar to the Arab in type, the Tersk breed was almost lost in the early twentieth century. More Arab blood was then introduced to maintain the type.

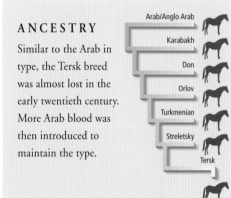

Arab/Anglo Arab
Karabakh
Don
Orlov
Turkmenian
Streletsky
Tersk

Back
Strong with muscular loins and rather flat croup

Mane and tail
The hair is generally sparse and very fine, the tail is carried high like that of an Arab

Head
Refined and Arabian in appearance, with large, expressive eyes

Neck
Muscular and high-set, with sloping shoulders

Three Tersk Horses driven to a traditional Russian troika. The horse in the center trots, the outside two canter to keep up.

Legs
Fine and lean with well-defined tendons, although rather light in bone

Tersk Horses coursing. Despite its rather fragile appearance, the Tersk possesses considerable stamina as well as speed. It is used as both a racehorse and as an endurance horse.

ORLOV TROTTER

Perhaps Russia's most famous breed, the Orlov Trotter was developed by Count Alexei Orlov at his Khrenov Stud as a carriage horse and racing trotter. The Count was presented with a gray Arab stallion called Smetanka, whose son Polkan I sired the foundation stallion, Bars I. Bars was bred to Arab, Dutch, Danish, and English mares, and the progeny was interbred until a fixed character was established to become the Orlov Trotter. Today, these horses are still bred at the Khrenov Stud, although variations of the breed can be found elsewhere. American Standardbred blood was introduced in the late nineteenth century—many believe to the breed's detriment—but efforts were made to retain the original's characteristics. It remains Russia's superlative trotting horse.

THE FACTS	
Origin	Russia
Color	predominantly gray
Height	17 hands (1.73 m)
Physique	small, straight head, long neck, wide chest, long back, good legs
Features	powerful, sound, enduring
Temperament	intelligent, quiet, willing
Use	trotting, competition, pleasure, harness

The Orlov Trotter was developed by Count Alexei Orlov at his Khrenov Stud at Voronezh in southwestern Russia, not far from the Ukraine and located either side of the river of the same name.

ANCESTRY

Bars I, a mix of Danish, Dutch, and Arab blood, is credited with being the foundation sire of the Orlov Trotter.

Arab
Don
Thoroughbred
Standardbred
Orlov Trotter

Head
Small and elegant, with straight profile

Quarters
Well-muscled and strong

Back
Rather long and straight

Neck
Long and swanlike, set high on the shoulders

Tail
Well-set and carried high

Legs
Well-made, with particularly powerful hindlegs for impressive impulsion

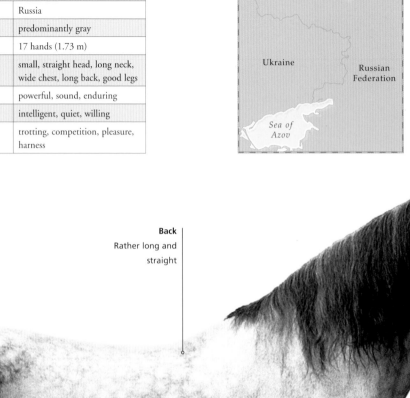

Orlov Trotters are usually gray, although black, bay, and chestnut coloring is also seen.

With its flashy good looks and extravagant, ground-covering stride, the Orlov Trotter is a popular harness horse, but is still most in demand as a racing trotter.

SORRAIA

It is hard to believe this unprepossessing breed was to form the foundation of the mighty Iberian kings, the Andalusian and Lusitano. Indigenous to the Iberian Peninsula, its name comes from the two rivers, Sor and Raia, that run through Portugal and Spain in the region in which this diminutive horse was discovered. The hardy Sorraia was used principally to herd the wild bulls of Iberia, to which its agility and courage made it ideally suited. It bears a strong resemblance to the primitive Tarpan and Przewalski's Horse, not least in its dun or grullo (gray–dun) coloring with black points and "zebra" striping. Sorraia foals are born with a zebra-like pattern all over. Sorraia DNA has been found in American Mustangs, where the distinctive grullo coloring still sometimes occurs.

THE FACTS	
Origin	Spain and Portugal
Color	dun or grullo
Height	14 hands (1.42 m)
Physique	convex head, short, strong neck, long back, sloping croup, low-set tail
Features	hardy, tough, brave
Temperament	eager to please, intelligent, gentle
Use	harness, riding

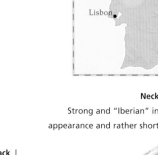

The Sorraia name derives from the Rivers Sor and Raia, which flow through the Iberian Peninsula and on whose plains the original equine grazed. Conditions were harsh and forage minimal.

Back
Primitive coloring of gray-dun, often with zebra stripes on the legs, dorsal or eel stripe along the back

Back
Long, with a sloping croup, and low-set tail

Neck
Strong and "Iberian" in appearance and rather short

Head
Pretty with Arab influences, convex profile is sometimes seen

Mane and tail
Black at the tips and stands upright, another primitive feature

Shoulders
Tend to be rather upright, giving the breed a short, choppy stride

Sorraias at grass in Portugal—the breed is extremely tough and hardy, and able to survive on meager rations.

Legs
Long and straight, with well-defined tendons

78

The "primitive" grullo or gray-dun coloring of the Sorraia is seen in Przewalski's Horse, to which the breed bears a strong resemblance

Iberian characteristics can be seen in the Sorraia, which, despite its small stature, is considered a horse rather than a pony.

ANDALUSIAN

This ancient breed originating in Spain continues to have universal appeal. The origins of an Iberian horse date back to about 25,000 B.C. Trade later brought oriental breeds into the peninsula and into the breed. These early Spanish horses were used by the cavalries of both the Greeks and the Romans. During the Renaissance the riding academies began to take an interest in the breed. For centuries it was favored by the European aristocracy. The Andalusian was nearly wiped out in the early nineteenth century by cross-breeding and the Napoleonic Wars. It survived largely because of the efforts of Carthusian monks in Jerez, Seville, and Castello. Many other breeds have benefited from the genetic influence of the Andalusian. It was spread throughout the New World by the Conquistadores, and consequently the Appaloosa, Mustang, and Quarter Horse, among others, have Andalusian ancestors.

THE FACTS

Origin	Andalusia, Spain
Color	usually gray, but also black, bay and chestnut
Height	16 hands (1.63 m)
Physique	broad head with convex profile; strong, arched neck; deep, short body; rounded hindquarters; short cannon bone
Features	elegant, athletic, animated
Temperament	intelligent, calm
Use	cavalry, Haute Ecole dressage, parades, bull-fighting

Spain has long been the breeding ground for some of the best horses in the world. The Portuguese Lusitano is descended from the Andalusian, as are the Lipizzaner stallions of Vienna's famous Spanish Riding School. From the mid-nineteenth century until 1962, no Andalusians could be exported from Spain.

ANCESTRY

The Andalusian breed developed in Spain from native species and the horses that accompanied the hordes of peoples crossing the region for trade and conquest.

Garrano
Noriker
Barb
Arab
Andalusian

The Andalusian is known for its courage and is the horse of choice for rejoneadores, mounted bull-fighters.

Mane
Long and luxuriant

Withers
Round and prominent

Neck
Powerful and arched providing balance

Shoulders
Long and sloping

Movement
Dazzling high-stepping action

Legs
Fine with short cannon bones

The Andalusian is one of the oldest and most sought-after breeds in the world. Its dramatic appearance makes it highly prized for parades.

LUSITANO

There are those who believe the Lusitano to be more "pure" than the Andalusian, whose Arab blood can be seen in its lighter, more concave profile. The Lusitano has a pronounced Roman nose, but is still an attractive breed and bears many similarities to its Spanish cousin. Certainly, the two are both Iberian horses, and have a high percentage of Barb and Sorraia blood. The Lusitano was developed for military use and for carriage driving, but is also highly prized by the rejoneador, the Portuguese bull-fighter. Its speed, agility, and calm temperament make it supremely suited to the bullring, in which it is considered a great dishonor if the rejoneador allows his horse to be injured. The Lusitano's agility and good looks also make it a natural choice for the dressage arena, where it can show off its balance, poise, and elevated paces.

THE FACTS	
Origin	Portugal
Color	all solid colors, including dun
Height	16 hands (1.63 m)
Physique	convex profile, wide forehead, arched, muscular neck, short back, good legs, abundant mane and tail
Features	agile, sturdy, robust
Temperament	calm, unflappable, brave
Use	riding, bull-fighting, dressage, harness

The Lusitano originated in Portugal and takes its name from the ancient Roman province that encompassed most of modern Portugal. Although ancient, the breed has only been known as the Lusitano since 1966.

ANCESTRY

Like the Andalusian, the Lusitano has its roots in the Sorraia, which can be seen in the "primitive" dun coloring that sometimes occurs.

Barb
Sorraia
Lusitano

While the Andalusian is predominantly gray in color, all solid colors are found in the Lusitano.

Head
Convex, hawk-like profile with large, intelligent eyes

Mane and tail
Silky and abundant

Back
Long, with strong and rounded croup, slightly slanting

Shoulders
Long and slanting

Chest
Medium size, but deep and muscular

Legs
The hindlegs have short thighs and large, strong hocks

Feet
Very hard and sound

Right, clockwise from left:
The Lusitano is an attractive horse, with considerable width across the forehead and bold, intelligent eyes.

Lusitano youngstock in Brazil—the breed is revered worldwide.

Lorenzo, the Flying Frenchman, and his team of Lusitano Horses appearing at the London International Horse Show in 2008.

ALTER-REAL

Although the breed lacks the beauty of the Andalusian and the nobility of the Lusitano, all three are closely related. The Alter-Real was established by the Portuguese Braganza dynasty to provide the royal family with superior horses for carriage driving and classical equitation. The breed was founded on 300 mares, probably Andalusian, imported from the Jerez region of Spain, and a national stud was established in Alter do Chão, which was to give the breed its name. The Alter-Real has something of a checkered past and during the Napoleonic invasion was disastrously diffused with Norman, Arab, Thoroughbred, and Hanoverian blood. Infusions later of Arab blood did not have the desired effect and it was only when further Andalusian lines were introduced that the breed was stabilized once more.

The Facts	
Origin	Portugal
Color	bay, brown, gray, occasionally chestnut
Height	16 hands (1.63 m)
Physique	medium-sized head with straight or convex profile, muscular, arched neck, pronounced wither, compact body, good legs
Features	strong, agile, hardy
Temperament	calm, intelligent, willing
Use	riding, competition

Established by the House of Braganza, the national stud at Alter do Chão was to provide exceptional riding and carriage horses for the Royal stables at Lisbon—"real" is the Portuguese word for "royal." This area of Portugal is still famous for its horse breeding.

ANCESTRY

The Alter-Real has had a checkered history but the bloodlines are now being carefully managed. Today the breed is rare, but not endangered.

Andalusian
Thoroughbred
Arab
Andalusian
Alter-Real

An Alter-Real performs the courbette, an "air above the ground" most usually seen in the Spanish Riding School of Vienna.

Neck
Muscular and arched, but rather short and carried high

Body
Compact with a short back, muscular hindquarters

Withers
Tends to be pronounced

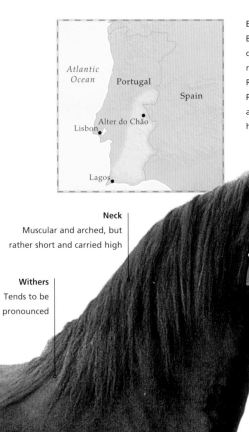

Head
Of medium size, with straight or convex profile, with a definite Iberian appearance

Legs
Slender but strong, with sturdy cannon bones and pasterns, well-positioned hocks

The Alter-Real lacks the beauty and nobility of its Iberian cousins, but it is still an attractive horse and a quick learner.

LIPIZZANER

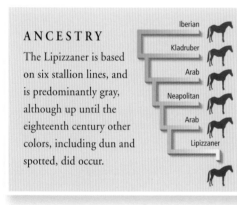

Famed as the dancing white horses of Vienna, the Lipizzaner takes its name from the original stud at Lipica (once Lipizza), in Slovenia, founded in 1580 by Archduke Charles II of Austria. Stallions imported from the Iberian Peninsula were used on the local Karst horses—small and predominantly white, they were tough small horses with a high-stepping, showy gait. The aim was to create a flashy white horse for the court stables in Vienna, for both classical riding and carriage driving. The breed is based on six foundation stallions, whose lines still exist today—they were a mix of Arab, Spanish, and Kladruber. Thoroughbred blood was later introduced, although it was deemed unsuccessful, and more Arab blood has since been added.

THE FACTS

Origin	Austria
Color	predominantly gray
Height	16 hands (1.63 m)
Physique	neat head, short, muscular neck, flat wither, sloping shoulder, long back, strong legs
Features	long-lived, late-maturing, powerful
Temperament	intelligent, gentle, trainable
Use	classical equitation, riding, harness, dressage

The Lipizzaner takes its name from the village of Lipica—Lipizza in Italian—in the Karst region of south-western Slovenia, extending into north-eastern Italy. It was developed in the sixteenth century with the support of the Habsburg nobility.

ANCESTRY

The Lipizzaner is based on six stallion lines, and is predominantly gray, although up until the eighteenth century other colors, including dun and spotted, did occur.

Iberian
Kladruber
Arab
Neapolitan
Arab
Lipizzaner

Mane
Short, muscular, and crested, with flattish wither

Body
Long back, with rounded hindquarters and well-set tail

Head
Large with straight profile, sometimes slightly convex

Shoulders
Deep and sloping, well suited to harness

Legs
Short and strong, well-muscled with plenty of bone, good, hard feet

Lipizzaners at the federal stud at Piber, in the Styrian Mountains in Austria.

Right, clockwise from top left:
The stallions perform in the baroque splendor of the Spanish Riding School.

Performing "airs above the ground" at the Spanish Riding School of Vienna.

An Austrian shepherd calls in a herd of Lipizzaner with a bugle.

A handler with a Lipizzaner stallion in New York City.

FRIESIAN

Paintings by the Dutch old masters depict strong, proud black horses carrying knights into battle—these were undoubtedly Friesians. The Friesian was the choice of kings, with its splendid extravagant action and noble bearing. A handsome animal, it is also extremely strong for its comparatively small size. It is believed to be descended from the primitive Forest Horse, and originated in the Friesland area of The Netherlands. During the Spanish occupation of 1568–1648, some Iberian blood was probably introduced for further refinement. In turn, the Friesian has played a role in other world breeds— its influence can be seen in the Dales and Fell Ponies of northern England; the Old Black Midland Horse, which was to become the Shire; the Dole of Norway; and the Oldenburger of Germany.

The Facts	
Origin	The Netherlands
Color	black
Height	15 hands (1.52 m)
Physique	noble head with straight or convex profile, muscular neck and shoulders, compact body, short, strong legs, hard feet
Features	noble, powerful, hardy
Temperament	kind, docile, amenable
Use	harness, light agricultural

Regarded as The Netherlands' only native breed, there are records of this sturdy black horse in the region from which it takes its name since the thirteenth century. Its influence stretches far and wide.

Neck
Of medium length and well-muscled, powerful

Topline
Although lighter in build than its predecessors, the modern Friesian has an impressive topline

Head
Noble profile, straight or slightly convex

The Friesian has the same abundant mane and tail as the Iberian breeds, whose blood was introduced for refinement. It is cheap to keep and possesses a cheerful willingness of character.

Mane and tail
Abundant and silky

Legs
Short and strong, with good bone and hard feet, some feather

Right: The Friesian sport horse stallion Satriani.

Inset: Small and compact, the Friesian is always black.

FREDERIKSBORG

King Frederik II of Denmark founded this elegant breed that bears his name in the 1560s. He imported horses from Spain and Italy to cross with the native Danish stock with the aim of producing handsome but powerful horses for the cavalry and the royal carriages. By the eighteenth century, the stud was producing two discernible types: a light riding horse with flowing, supple action, and a heavier-built carriage horse. The latter were bred to be of similar color and size so they could be driven in matched teams of six or eight. The breed was almost a victim of its own success—so many were exported that they almost vanished from their native land. The stud closed in 1849, but enough breeders retained their horses that, with infusions of Friesian, Oldenburg, Thoroughbred, and Arab blood, the Frederiksborg was revitalized in the twentieth century.

THE FACTS	
Origin	Denmark
Color	chestnut with some white markings
Height	16 hands (1.63 m)
Physique	large, straight head, arched neck, medium-length back, long legs
Features	strong, elegant, supple
Temperament	calm, even, willing
Use	riding, harness

The Frederiksborg takes its name from the Royal Frederiksborg Stud founded in 1562. Frederiksborg is not far from Copenhagen, on the island of Zealand.

Two types of Frederiksborg were developed at the Royal Stud, and both were bred to be elegant and reliable, whether ridden or put to a carriage.

Andalusian
Native Danish
Friesian
Oldenburg
Thoroughbred
Arab
Frederiksborg

Coat
Always chestnut, with flaxen mane and tail

Back
A little long with powerful hindquarters

Neck
Strong and well-arched, set on a low wither and sloping shoulders

Head
Quite large with a straight profile, but undeniably handsome

Legs
Long but well in proportion, with good, well-formed joints, and small, hard feet

The Frederiksborg was bred as a carriage horse, so it was important that it could be matched—all Frederiksborg horses are chestnut.

Three Frederiksborg stallions, Hjelm, Rex Bregneb, and Tito Naesdal, play-fighting.

KNABSTRUP

A Spanish cavalry mare was to form the basis of this Danish breed. It is thought she was left behind by an officer during the Napoleonic wars and was bought by a butcher named Flaebe. The mare, chestnut with some white in her coat, was thereafter known as Flaebenhoppen, which means "Flaebe's mare." The name Knabstrup, or Knabstruper, comes from the estate owned a Major Villars Lunn, who bought the original mare to found the breed. Bred to a Frederiksborg stallion, she passed on both her unusual coloring and sweet temper. All her offspring had the spotted coat, similar to that of the American Appaloosa, and her grandson, Mikkel, is credited as the breed's foundation sire. It is now considered a rare breed, but its gentle nature and distinctive coat give it an enduring popularity.

THE FACTS	
Origin	Denmark
Color	spotted
Height	16 hands (1.63 m)
Physique	small, refined head, medium length of rein, compact body, good feet
Features	sound, strong, tough
Temperament	gentle, trainable, willing
Use	riding, competition, harness

The breed is named for the stud at Knabstrupgaard estate in Holbæk, a city in Region Zealand, Denmark. The stud was founded in 1812 based on the mare Flaebenhoppen, purchased by the estate's owner.

ANCESTRY

The Knabstrup's extravagantly spotted coat was sometimes seen in prehistoric Iberian horses from which the breed ultimately derives.

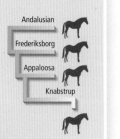

Andalusian
Frederiksborg
Appaloosa
Knabstrup

Coat
Striking and distinctive, usually white with brown or black spots, although other variations occur

Body
Compact and strong with muscular quarters

Neck
Tends to be rather short, but is strong and well-muscled

Head
Well-proportioned with a pleasing expression

Legs
Proportionate and well-made, with good bone, and strong feet

It is easy to see from its striking coat why this Knabstrup was christened Confetti.

Right, clockwise from left:
The spotted coat of this Knabstrup stands out against the snow.

The Spanish influence can be seen in this elegant horse's noble head.

A range of different coat patterns are seen in the Knabstrup.

OLDENBURG

The heaviest of the German warmbloods, the Oldenburg was developed by a renowned horseman named Herzob Anton Gunther von Oldenburg in the seventeenth century. The breed is based on Friesian stock and using Neapolitan, Turkish, Spanish, and Barb lines. The original aim was to produce a powerful and handsome carriage horse but later infusions of Thoroughbred, Cleveland Bay, and Hanoverian blood have produced an elegant but strong equine, easy to train and possessing dynamic paces. Refining Thoroughbred blood has given the breed considerable beauty, while its Friesian origins can still be seen in its noble bearing. It excels in the show jumping ring, the dressage arena, and across country.

THE FACTS	
Origin	Germany
Color	predominantly black, dark bay, brown, gray
Height	16.3 hands (1.70 m)
Physique	noble head, well-set neck on good wither, sloping shoulder, muscular quarters, excellent legs and feet
Features	muscular, powerful, strong
Temperament	kind, willing, gentle
Use	competition, harness

Based on the Dutch Friesian horse, the Oldenburg was developed on stock living between the Weser River in Germany and The Netherlands. It was named after a tiny former kingdom in Lower Saxony.

ANCESTRY

A gray stallion named Kranich, of Spanish origin, was important in the early development of the Oldenburg breed, while East Friesian blood gave it substance.

Friesian
Neapolitan
Turkish
Barb
Andalusian
Thoroughbred
Oldenburg

Neck
Well-set with medium length of rein, well-formed wither

Back
Long side for a sport horse, with wide, powerful quarters

Head
Handsome and noble, with a convex profile and kind eye

Shoulders
Strong and sloping, although not as long as those of the Thoroughbred

Chest
Deep and wide with plenty of heart room

Legs
Clean and hard, with generous joints and around 9 inches (23 cm) of bone

Feet
In proportion to the horse's frame, well-formed and sound

Canada's Jill Henselwood and the Oldenburg Special Ed competing in the show jumping final at the 2008 Beijing Olympics.

Right: Pinto Oldenburg mare and foal, in Texas.

Far right: Although a heavier warmblood breed, the Oldenburg is handsome, as illustrated by this stallion, Rubaiyat.

EINSIEDLER

Sometimes referred to as the Swiss Anglo–Norman or Swiss Half-Bred, the Einsiedler is an enduring all-purpose warmblood. It is thought to have been in existence since the tenth century, and was first established at the Benedictine Abbey of Einsiedeln. It was founded on local stock, called Schwyer Horses, and the first studbook was opened in 1655. A more comprehensive studbook was compiled in 1784 by Father Isidor Moser. The breed was improved by using Anglo–Norman mares and a Yorkshire Coach Horse stallion, named Bracken, which was imported in 1865. Further infusions of Swedish, Anglo–Norman, and Holstein blood have refined and defined Switzerland's warmblood, which today are performance tested at three and again at five. Horses are selected for breeding only if their pedigree includes proven performance horses.

THE FACTS

Origin	Switzerland
Color	all solid colors
Height	16.2 hands (1.68 m)
Physique	refined head, muscular neck, good shoulders, strong body, powerful quarters, excellent legs, good feet
Features	sound, strong, good-looking
Temperament	calm, willing, easy-going
Use	competition

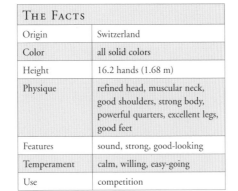

There is a long tradition of horse breeding by the world's monasteries and this warmblood takes its name from the Benedictine Monastery of Einsiedeln, Switzerland, where it was first established. It is still performance tested in the land of its birth.

ANCESTRY

Sometimes called the Swiss Half-Blood—or Schweizer Halbblut—the Einsiedler was founded on native Swiss stock.

Schwyer (native Swiss)
Anglo-Norman
Yorkshire Coach Horse
Holstein
Einsiedler

A handsome Einsiedler in full harness

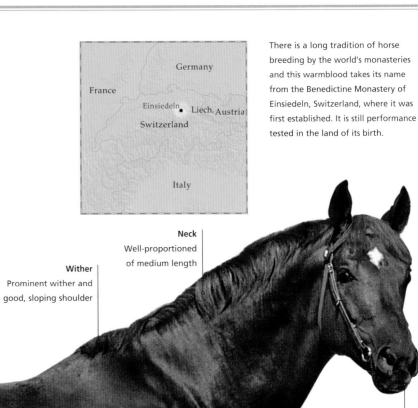

Back
Muscular and powerful, giving the breed its natural athleticism

Wither
Prominent wither and good, sloping shoulder

Neck
Well-proportioned of medium length

Head
Handsome head, straight or slightly convex profile

Legs
Long and clean, with well-defined tendons and good joints

Right, clockwise from top left:
The Einsiedler is a proven all-round sport horse, suitable for all equestrian disciplines.

The Einsiedler mare Myrta, with her foal, and the Kloster Einsiedeln in the background

The breed has a natural athleticism, seen in most warmbloods.

GELDERLANDER

Given its varied influences, it is astonishing that the Gelderlander has remained a fixed type. Originally bred as a light farm horse, it was the result of crossing local breeds, notably the Friesian, with Thoroughbred, Anglo–Norman, Hackney, and Oldenburg. The resulting horse was suitable for light agricultural work, and also made a handsome, high-stepping carriage horse. It was also widely used in the army, both as a cavalry mount and for pulling heavy artillery. Later infusions of Arabian and further Thoroughbred blood have straightened the horse's profile—although the Roman convex nose does still appear—and Orlov Trotter influences have given it more speed. Like many warmbloods, it has a superb jump, and is also becoming popular in the dressage arena. It remains, however, a talented carriage horse, and is often seen in international competitions.

THE FACTS

Origin	The Netherlands
Color	chestnut, gray
Height	16 hands (1.63 m)
Physique	straight or slightly convex profile, medium neck, good shoulders, long back, powerful quarters, high-set tail, clean legs
Features	extravagant gait, versatile, powerful
Temperament	quiet, kind, willing
Use	harness, competition

The province of Gelderland in the central eastern region of The Netherlands has long been associated with the breeding of superlative horses, and its eponymous warmblood is worthy of the name.

ANCESTRY

The breed's draught heritage from the East Friesian is evident in its Roman nose, but Thoroughbred and Arab blood has refined it.

Dutch Friesian
East Friesian
Thoroughbred
Anglo-Norman
Hackney
Oldenburg
Gelderlander

The Gelderlander is predominantly chestnut in color, although some grays and the occasional bay do occur.

Head
Lean and refined, with large, expressive eyes

Neck
Medium in length and well-muscled

Back
Long, with generous quarters, straight in the croup

Shoulders
Strong and sloping, although not as long as those of the Thoroughbred

Legs
Very clean, plenty of good, hard bone, excellent feet

Right, clockwise from top left:
A smart Gelderlander in harness, competing at a show in Bilthoven in The Netherlands.

A Dutch handler puts a Gelderlander through its paces.

A team of Gelderlanders doing what they were bred for, harnessed to a handsome carriage.

DUTCH WARMBLOOD

A fairly new breed, the Dutch Warmblood is already widely recognized as a superlative competition horse. It owes much to both the Gelderlander and Groningen, on which it is founded. Beginning in the 1950s, Dutch breeders strove to select the best from each for their breeding programs, then added Thoroughbred blood for refinement, speed, and scope. Oldenburg and Hanoverian blood was later introduced to enhance the breed's conformation and temperament. The Dutch Warmblood is a handsome, athletic, and sound equine powerhouse, with excellent paces, great jumping ability, and a calm, eager-to-please temperament. Today, the Dutch Warmblood studbook recognizes three types of Dutch Warmblood—the harness horse, the heavier Gelderland type, and the all-round sport horse.

THE FACTS	
Origin	The Netherlands
Color	all solid colors
Height	16.2 hands (1.68 m)
Physique	straight, sometimes rather plain head, medium-length neck, good shoulders, well-defined wither, long back, excellent legs
Features	athletic, strong, sound
Temperament	eager, calm, willing
Use	competition

Combining the Gelderlander with the Groningen produced a horse of great strength and soundness, suitable for light agricultural work in The Netherlands, where farmers relied heavily on their horses for working the clay or sandy soil.

ANCESTRY

Denmark's supreme sport horse is based on the country's two native breeds, the Groningen and the Gelderlander.

Groningen
Gelderlander
Thoroughbred
Hanoverian
Oldenburg
Dutch Warmblood

The Dutch Warmblood Class Action lets off some steam.

Back
Rather straight and quite long, but well-made

Head
Fine and clean-cut, exceptionally good looking and noble

Shoulders
Powerful and muscular, with plenty of slope to give it its free-flowing stride

Chest
Deep and wide, providing good heart room for the horse's "engine"

Clockwise from top left:
Christina Liebherr of Switzerland
competing the Dutch Warmblood
LB Robin Hood at Aachen, Germany,
in 2008.

Jodie Stevens Kelly shows off her
Dutch Warmblood Manhattan's
dressage ability at West Palm Beach,
Florida.

American Steffen Peters competes
the Dutch Warmblood stallion
Ravel in the dressage at the Olympic
Games in Beijing.

Pablo, a strikingly marked Dutch
Warmblood.

GRONINGEN

Originally developed as a light agricultural horse, the Groningen was almost overtaken by the breed it helped to establish, the Dutch Warmblood, such was the success of the latter. In the 1970s, the Dutch Warmblood had almost absorbed all Groningens and only one pure-bred stallion remained, called Baldewijn. Oldenburg blood was introduced to help to re-establish the breed. Thoroughbred and Hanoverian blood was later added to keep the type without compromising it. Bigger than either the Gelderlander or Dutch Warmblood, it is a powerful, muscular warmblood type. While not as flashy as its Gelderland neighbor, it is reliable and possesses great stamina. Today, there are only about 300 Groningens remaining and each August, the breed has its own national show to ensure only the best are used for continuing the line.

THE FACTS	
Origin	The Netherlands
Color	black, bay, brown
Height	16.2 hands (1.68 m)
Physique	plain head, short neck, long back, strong quarters, round joints
Features	strong, reliable, sound
Temperament	calm, willing, kind
Use	harness, riding

Groningen is the northeastern-most province of The Netherlands, bordered in the north by the Wadden Sea. The horse that bears its name needed to be sound and powerful to work the heavy clay soil.

Neck
Short and powerful, set on fairly high

Quarters
Broad and well-muscled

Topline
Substantial and level, rectangular frame

Head
Plain and notably convex

Legs
Strong with good, hard bone, rather round, fleshy joints, with broad, sound feet

A Groningen mare and foal, pictured in Holland.

A powerful breed, the Groningen has a correct walk and an expressive trot, and although it is heavily built, it still has quality.

HANOVERIAN

Germany's most successful equine export is perhaps the benchmark of all European warmblood breeds. This is a horse that ticks all the boxes—handsome, elegant, athletic, and trainable, it excels in all equestrian disciplines. The eighteenth century founding stallions included 14 black Holsteiners bred to native draft mares thus founding the Hanoverian breed. Initially bred as a carriage and cavalry horse, the aim was to produce a slightly lighter, more quality animal, suitable also for riding and light agricultural work. Thoroughbred blood was introduced to this end. The Hanoverian was almost wiped out by the Napoleonic wars of 1812–13 and, by 1816, there were just 30 stallions remaining. The breed was stabilized with more Thoroughbred blood, plus some Trakehner to ensure it did not become too light.

THE FACTS	
Origin	Germany
Color	all solid colors
Height	16.2 hands (1.68 m)
Physique	attractive head set on long neck, sloping shoulder, wide, deep chest, long back, broad quarters, good legs with plenty of bone
Features	strong, sound, powerful
Temperament	equable, willing, intelligent
Use	competition

Germany's supreme warmblood was developed at the state stud of Lower Saxony in Calle. The stud was founded in 1735 by George II, Elector of Hanover and King of England.

ANCESTRY

The success of crossing English Thoroughbreds with native German stock produced a superlative warmblood.

Holstein

Thoroughbred

Trakehner

Hanoverian

Head
Light for a warmblood, and very elegant

Neck
Long and fine, with a prominent wither

Quarters
Muscled and well-shaped, flat croup, high-set tail

Body
Deep and powerful, well-sprung ribs, medium-length back

Shoulders
Good, sloping shoulders, allowing for the breed's superb paces

Legs
Exceptional legs, with excellent bone, and sound joints

Feet
Formerly a weakness, now hard and well-made

The Hanoverian's good looks are matched by its perfect temperament.

The Hanoverian has excellent gaits, including an elastic, ground-covering walk, a floating trot, and a rhythmic canter, which makes it excel in all sporting arenas.

HOLSTEIN

When the monks of a monastry at Uetersen were given permission to graze their horses on private land in 1285, they repaid the favor by breeding a heavy but elegant horse. Founded on German, Spanish, and Oriental blood, the horse was developed for agriculture in the Schleswig-Holstein area, from which it took its name. Handsome and powerful, it was also used as a cavalry horse and for pulling heavy artillery. Later, it became popular as a carriage horse, although it was rather heavy, with a short stride. During the nineteenth century, the breed was lightened with some Thoroughbred blood, and Yorkshire Coach Horse lines were introduced to lengthen the stride. Further Thoroughbred blood refined the breed after the Second World War, and today's Holstein is a handsome, talented, and exceptionally athletic sport horse.

THE FACTS

Origin	Germany
Color	predominantly bay
Height	17 hands (1.73 m)
Physique	attractive head, muscular, elegant neck, sloping shoulder, deep chest, muscular quarters, strong legs
Features	sturdy, athletic, versatile
Temperament	easy-going, willing, kind
Use	competition

In the thirteenth century, Gerhard, Count of Holstein and Storman, granted grazing rights to the monastery at Ueterson, in Schleswig-Holstein in northern Germany. There, the monks developed the Holstein breed.

ANCESTRY

Holsteins were originally bred as warhorses, but Thoroughbred blood has refined the breed and given it more quality.

Oriental
Andalusian
German stock
Thoroughbred
Yorkshire Coach Horse
Holstein

Body
Much less heavy than its predecessors, thanks to more Thoroughbred blood

Head
Straight, showing the Thoroughbred influence

Shoulders
Nicely sloping, allowing for good paces, clearly defined wither

Legs
Strong and generally sound, good bone

The Holstein stallion Riverman, pictured in Maryland, U.S.A

Right, clockwise from top left:
The modern Holstein is predominantly bay in color.

Peter Eriksson of Sweden competing the Holstein VDL Cardento at the All-England Jumping Course at Hickstead.

A Holstein foal in Texas. The breed has a devoted following in the United States.

Bin Zhang, jumping for the home nation, at the 2008 Olympic Games in Beijing on the Holstein, Coertis.

SELLE FRANCAIS

France's warmblood is the epitome of a sport horse—it has good looks, superb paces, elastic movement, and innate jumping ability. The Selle Francais Baloubet De Rouet won three consecutive World Show Jumping Championships (1998–2000) and a silver medal at the 2004 Athens Olympic Games. The breed was developed in the nineteenth century at the state stud farms at Saint Lo and Le Pin in Normandy by crossing local stock with English Thoroughbred and Norfolk Trotters. Two distinct types resulted—the French Trotter and the Anglo–Norman. The latter also developed into two strains, a heavier draft type and a lighter riding type. More Thoroughbred blood, notably a stallion named Orange Peel, was added, with Anglo Arab and Arab, to refine the riding type to become "le Cheval de Selle Francais," or French Saddle Horse.

THE FACTS	
Origin	France
Color	all solid colors
Height	17 hands (1.73 m)
Physique	attractive head, long neck, sloping shoulder, deep chest, long body, strong legs
Features	energetic, intelligent, fast
Temperament	tractable, willing, even-tempered
Use	competition

The Selle Francais was developed at the studs of Saint Lo and Le Pin in Normandy, and is a comparatively new warmblood breed. It was given its full name—"le Cheval de Selle Francais"—in 1958, and the studbook was opened in 1965.

ANCESTRY

The Selle Francais is the product of a government breeding program in Normandy during the nineteenth century and is a superb sport horse.

French stock
Thoroughbred
Norfolk Trotter
Anglo Arab
Arab
Selle Francais

Spain's Paola Amilibia Puig show jumping on the Selle Francais Cabri D'Elle at the 2007 European Championships in Mannheim, Germany.

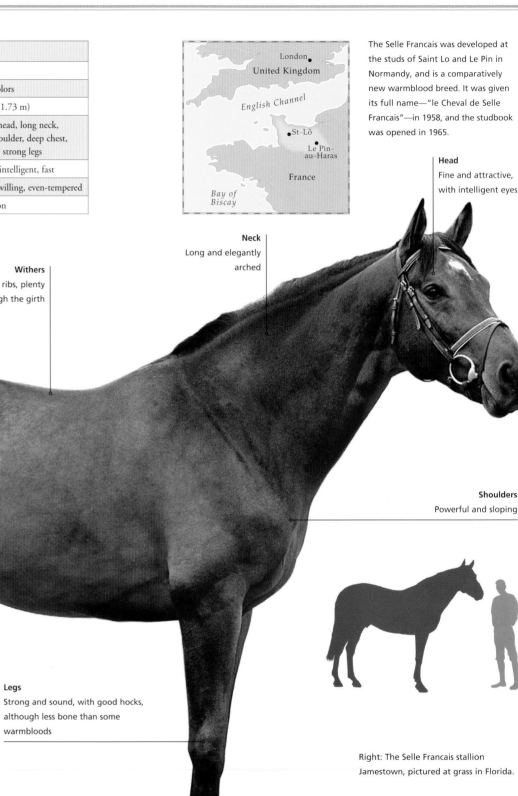

Head
Fine and attractive, with intelligent eyes

Neck
Long and elegantly arched

Withers
Deep chest, well-sprung ribs, plenty of room through the girth

Shoulders
Powerful and sloping

Legs
Strong and sound, with good hocks, although less bone than some warmbloods

Right: The Selle Francais stallion Jamestown, pictured at grass in Florida.

Far right: Nicolas Touzaint and the Selle Francais Hildago De Lile, on whom he won the world-famous Badminton Horse Trials in 2008—the first Frenchman ever to do so.

TRAKEHNER

Bloodlines of this superb warmblood can be traced back to the East Prussian royal stud, established in 1732. Originally a strong, stocky native type of equine, the breed was lightened and refined with Arab and Thoroughbred blood in the early 1800s. The objective was to produce a quality riding horse to be used by the cavalry in wartime that was tough and strong enough to work the farms during periods of peace. The addition of small amounts of hot blood produced a substantial horse, with considerable power and plenty of bone, which was surprisingly refined. The modern Trakehner has lost none of these qualities—it stands up to 17 hands (1.73 m) and has great presence and bearing, as well as excellent paces.

THE FACTS

Origin	East Prussia
Color	all solid colors
Height	17 hands (1.73 m)
Physique	elegant head, long neck, sloping shoulder, muscular quarters, strong joints
Features	elegant, powerful
Temperament	keen, intelligent, eager to please
Use	competition, riding

This breed takes its name from the East Prussian royal stud located at Trakehnen, now part of Russia's Kaliningrad territory and known as Yasnaya Polyana.

ANCESTRY

The Trakehner was developed from native stock, which was probably descended from the Konik and the Tarpan that preceded it.

Native Prussian stock
Thoroughbred
Arab
Trakehner

Its light, floating trot and soft balanced canter mean the Trakehner excels in the dressage arena.

Quarters
Muscular and pleasantly rounded

Back
Of proportionate length and strong

Withers
Well-defined

Neck
Elegantly tapered with a good length of rein

Shoulders
Sloping to allow for freedom of movement

Tail
Set and carried high

Legs
Well-formed joints, clean and hard, and plenty of bone

Feet
Exceptionally sound, well-made

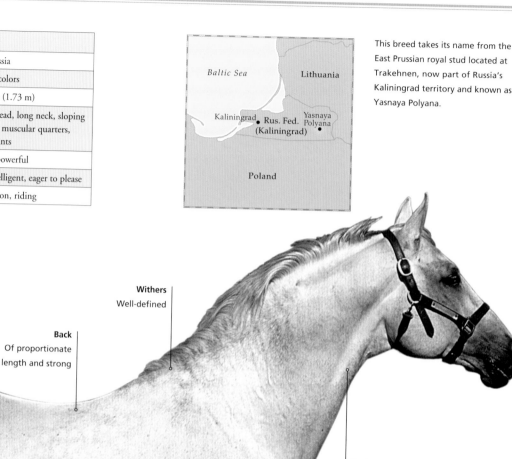

Thoroughbred influence can be seen in the Trakehner's refined head, with its straight profile and bold eye. The coarser Roman nose of the ancient stock has been bred out.

DANISH WARMBLOOD

Although Denmark has been a major player in the horse breeding world for centuries, her sport horse breed is relatively new. The noble Frederiksborg was to form the basis of this warmblood breed, which was initially called the Danish Sports Horse. When crossed with a Thoroughbred, the Frederiksborg produced a quality riding horse, with Thoroughbred good looks but more bone and substance. Later, infusions of Selle Francais, Trakehner, and Wielkopolski blood were added, together with more Thoroughbred blood for refinement. The Danish Warmblood is a substantial horse, standing up to 16.2 hands (1.65 m), and shares the equable temperament of most warmblood breeds. The studbook was opened in 1960, so it is one of the younger warmbloods, but it is already a star on the world's stage.

THE FACTS	
Origin	Denmark
Color	bay, brown, chestnut, black
Height	16.2 hands (1.68 m)
Physique	attractive, refined head, muscular neck, sloping shoulder, deep chest, strong back, clean legs
Features	tough, bold, courageous
Temperament	calm, intelligent, amenable
Use	competition, riding

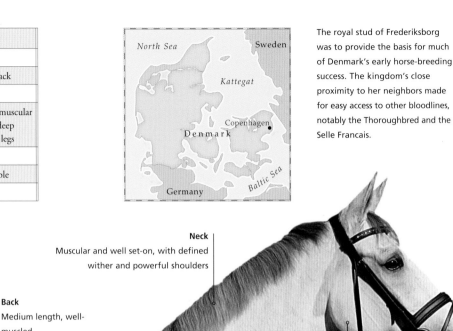

The royal stud of Frederiksborg was to provide the basis for much of Denmark's early horse-breeding success. The kingdom's close proximity to her neighbors made for easy access to other bloodlines, notably the Thoroughbred and the Selle Francais.

ANCESTRY

Based on the Frederiksborg, the Danish Warmblood has benefited from infusions of French, German, and Polish blood to produce a superlative sport horse.

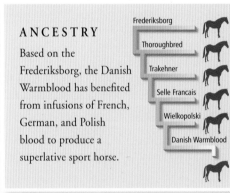

Frederiksborg
Thoroughbred
Trakehner
Selle Francais
Wielkopolski
Danish Warmblood

Neck
Muscular and well set-on, with defined wither and powerful shoulders

Quarters
Pleasingly rounded, powerful

Back
Medium length, well-muscled

Head
Handsome, with considerable quality

A natural athlete, the Danish Warmblood excels in the show jumping ring, possessing speed, stamina, and jumping ability.

Legs
Strong forearms, clean joints, ample bone

Movement
Naturally elevated paces

Feet
Excellent in shape and very sound

The modern Danish Warmblood is wiry and agile, with considerable endurance and movement, as well as an equable temperament.

BUDYONNY

Named for the Red Army's Marshall Budyonny—whose aim was to breed the perfect cavalry horse—the Russian warmblood is the result of crossing Thoroughbreds with Dons. As a cavalry mount, it needed to be fast and tough, as well as good-looking and trainable. Thoroughbred stallions were used on Don, as well as some Chernomor mares—similar to the Don but slightly smaller and lighter. Some Karabakh blood was also introduced, with less success. The breed was officially recognized in 1948—just a few years before the Russian cavalry was disbanded. Today, the Budyonny is still produced at the state studs, but some herds of them run free under the care of a groom, ensuring they remain tough and hardy. It is an attractive horse that shows its Thoroughbred influence, but has the calm, kind temperament of the warmblood.

THE FACTS	
Origin	Russia
Color	predominantly chestnut
Height	15.2 hands (1.57 m)
Physique	refined head, slightly concave profile, medium-length neck, sloping shoulder, muscular quarters, excellent legs with good bone
Features	athletic, trainable
Temperament	calm, intelligent
Use	competition, riding, harness

Marshall Budyonny helped to develop the breed at the military stud of Rostov northeast of Moscow. As well as at the state studs, the Budyonny today is bred in the Ukraine and in the area around the Black Sea.

ANCESTRY

Based on Thoroughbred stallions put to Don or Chermomor mares, the Budyonny was for some time known as the Anglo-Don.

Don
Thoroughbred
Chernomor
Karabakh
Budyonny

The Budyonny's refined head shows the Thoroughbred influence—the modern breed carries a greater proportion of Thoroughbred blood than the original "Anglo-Don."

Croup
Muscular and sloping

Body
Plenty of depth through the girth, well-made and proportionate

Head
Fine and neat, with tapered muzzle

Neck
Long and straight, but in proportion

Coat
Often has the iridescent gleam seen in both the Don and Karabakh

Legs
Slender and rather straight, with small, well-made feet

These four Budyonny Horses are pulling a tachanka—a horse drawn machinegun carriage used extensively by the Red Army in the early twentieth century.

WIELKOPOLSKI

Poland's warmblood is closely related to the Trakehner and as such perhaps does not get the recognition as a supreme sport horse that it deserves. It was developed using two Polish breeds, the Poznan and the Mazury, that are now extinct. The Poznan, a mix of Arab, Thoroughbred, Trakehner, and Hanoverian blood, was a versatile farm horse, used for both agricultural work and general riding. The Mazury, chiefly Trakehner in origin, was of more quality. When combined, the two produced a superlative athlete. Further infusions of Arab, Thoroughbred, and Anglo Arab blood have given the breed more refinement, and it is considered by many to be one of the best warmbloods in the world. It has already enjoyed considerable success in the dressage arena and the show jumping ring, and is increasingly in demand as an event horse for its innate jumping ability and natural athleticism.

THE FACTS	
Origin	Poland
Color	all solid colors
Height	16.2 hands (1.68 m)
Physique	straight head, intelligent eyes, long, elegant neck, sloping shoulder, deep chest, compact body, powerful quarters, long, clean legs
Features	athletic, powerful, good-looking
Temperament	intelligent, calm
Use	competition, riding

The Wielkopolski is based on the Poznan, which was bred around the town of that name, and the Mazury, which was bred at the Liski state stud in the northeast of the country. Today, the Wielkopolski is primarily bred in central and western Poland.

ANCESTRY

Based on two now extinct Polish breeds, the Wielkopolski is similar to the Trakehner and is an excellent sport horse

Mazury
Poznan
Arab
Thoroughbred
Hanoverian
Wielkopolski

The Wielkopolski is recognized as an excellent dressage horse, with natural balance and extravagant paces.

Quarters
Powerful and well-muscled

Body
Plenty of heart room, compact and strong with enough length in the back to give scope

Neck
Muscular and proportionate, well set-on

Head
A typically handsome warmblood head with a straight profile

Shoulders
Excellent sloping shoulder to give the horse long, smooth paces

Legs
Well-formed hindlegs ensure powerful jumping ability, plenty of bone

Feet
Well-made and hard

With its calm temperament, good looks, athleticism, and smooth, elastic paces, the Wielkopolski is Poland's best-kept secret.

MUSTANG

Mustangs have roamed across America for centuries, and they take their name from the Spanish word *mesteño* or *monstenco*, meaning "wild" or "stray." The Mustang is descended from the Spanish horses brought to the New World by the Conquistadors, probably a mix of Sorraia, Andalusian, Lusitano, and Alter-Real. But in the melting pot of the vast American plains, other breeds have since contributed to the Mustang, including those brought in by French settlers, and the heavy East Friesian horses purchased by the United States Government to pull heavy artillery. In the early twentieth century, there were an estimated two million Mustang, but as they had to share the plains with cattle and food was scarce, many were shot by ranchers. Today, the Mustang is protected by the Wild Free-Roaming Horse and Burro Act 1971.

THE FACTS	
Origin	U.S.A.
Color	all colors
Height	14 hands (1.42 m)
Physique	generally refined, intelligent head, medium length neck and back, clean legs, small, hard feet
Features	hardy, swift
Temperament	lively, intelligent
Use	wild horse

Descended from the Spanish stock brought by the Conquistadors, Mustang were once found all over North America, but are now mainly in the western states.

In 1977, small herds of dun horses were discovered in Oregon and were given the name Kiger Mustang. They are thought to be more "pure" than other feral herds, with apparent Spanish features.

Neck
Medium in length

Body
Generally compact

Head
Although the Mustang varies because of the mix of breeds, it usually has a refined head

Coat
The full range of coat colors is seen

Legs
Clean legs, with small hard feet

Wild Mustang are herded at Rock Spring Ranch in Bend, Oregon.

CHINCOTEAGUE

Romantic tales abound of shipwrecks and horses swimming ashore, but no one really knows the origins of the semi-feral ponies on the islands of Chincoteague and Assateague, off the coast of Virginia in North America. Made famous by Marguerite Henry's enduring tale *Misty of Chincoteague*, the ponies actually live on the larger island of Assateague, where they are divided into two herds—one at the Maryland end of the island, and one at the Virginia end. Each summer, the Virginia herd is rounded up and swum across the channel separating the islands by "saltwater cowboys" to the cheers and applause of thousands of spectators. Once on the island, the foals are auctioned off. The ponies survive on the unforgiving islands on meager rations and are tough and hardy, but gentle enough to make ideal mounts for children.

THE FACTS	
Origin	Virginia and Maryland, U.S.A.
Color	all colors
Height	12 hands (1.22 m)
Physique	neat, pretty head, medium-length neck, short back, thick mane and tail
Features	hardy, good doers
Temperament	gentle, kind, intelligent
Use	riding, harness

The ponies live on the island of Assateague and are managed by two agencies—the Virginia herd by the Chincoteague Volunteer Fire Department, and the Maryland herd by the National Park Service.

The Chincoteague varies considerably, with all coat colors occurring, but usually has a small, neat pony head.

Neck
Short and stocky

Coat
All colors are seen in the Chincoteague

Head
Small and neat

Legs
Generally rather weak, with poor joints and light bone

Forage on the island is of poor quality and salt laden, but it is said of the Chincoteague Pony that it can "grow fat on concrete."

MORGAN

It was once the tradition that a horse was known by the name of its master—and Justin Morgan's stallion was to found a breed of its own. There is little known about the origins of the original Morgan—he was thought to have Welsh Cob or Thoroughbred blood—but he was small and compact, and very tough. His name was Figure, and tales of his speed, beauty, strength, endurance, and gentle disposition soon spread around Randolph, Vermont, where its owner, a schoolteacher by trade, lived. As the New World expanded, so did the Morgan's popularity. Men answered the call of the Gold Rush on his back; the Vermont Cavalry rode him into the Civil War. The only survivor of the Battle of Little Big Horn was said to be a Morgan called Comanche. Figure died in 1821, but he left three sons—Sherman, Bulrush, and Woodbury—to continue the line of the Morgan horse.

THE FACTS	
Origin	Vermont, U.S.A.
Color	predominantly bay, black, brown, chestnut
Height	14.2 hands (1.47 m)
Physique	neat head, slightly concave profile, arched neck, well-defined wither, short back, well-sprung ribs, long croup, high-set tail, clean, sound legs with good, flat bone
Features	hardy, strong, alert
Temperament	gentle, eager, tractable
Use	riding competition, harness

The original "Justin Morgan Horse" was born in West Springfield, Massachusetts, but lived most of his life in Randolph, Vermont. Today, the Morgan is bred primarily in the southern states of America.

Neck
Of medium length, with well-defined wither

Back
Short, broad, and well-muscled

Quarters
Powerful and well-balanced

Head
Refined and full of quality, sometimes showing Arab characteristics

Shoulders
Strong and sloping

The Morgan has a fine, quality head, often with a slightly concave profile.

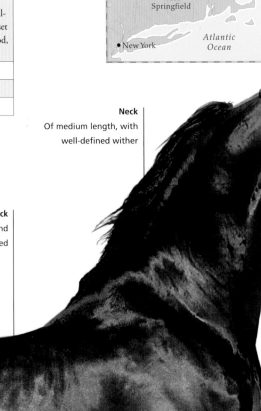

Stance
"Park out" stance ensures that carriage horses cannot move off suddenly when passengers are climbing in or out of a carriage

Legs
Proportionate, slender but with good bone

Feet
Generally good, round in shape, but often trimmed to enhance natural action

Young Morgan Horses at Dragonsmeade, Kentucky. The Morgan is the first documented American breed and has contributed to the Saddlebred and Standardbred.

PONY OF THE AMERICAS

Like the Morgan, the Pony of the Americas began with just one horse, named Black Hand. The result of an accidental mating between a Shetland and an Appaloosa-Arab, Black Hand belonged to a lawyer named Les Boomhower, who named the colt for the unusual marking on its quarters. Boomhower established a new registry in 1954—the Pony of the Americas Club—with stringent breed standards. No pony in the Club should stand higher than 13 hands, nor less than 11 hands; its head must be refined, with some "dishing;" it must have the conformation of the Quarter Horse; and—perhaps most importantly—must be spotted, like an Appaloosa. Black Hand was the first Pony of the Americas, and his legacy lives on—the "POA" is a good-looking, charming, gentle-natured American success story.

THE FACTS	
Origin	Iowa, U.S.A.
Color	spotted
Height	12 hands (1.22 m)
Physique	refined head, with concave profile, slightly arched neck, sloping shoulder, deep chest, short back, muscular quarters, clean, straight legs
Features	trainable, hardy
Temperament	gentle, intelligent
Use	ideal child's pony

The colt Black Hand, the first registered POA, was owned by Les Boomhower of Mason City, Iowa, who founded the Pony of the Americas Club in 1954. There are now more than 40 Clubs across the United States.

ANCESTRY

The founding colt, Black Hand, was the result of a mating between a Shetland and an Appaloosa-Arab cross. Other breeds have since been used in its development.

Appaloosa
Arab
Shetland
Welsh
Quarter Horse
Mustang
Pony of the Americas

It is a breed requirement that the spots on a POA should be visible from up to 40 feet (12 m) away.

Croup
Pleasantly sloping, tail carried at medium height

Body
Compact and short-coupled, typical "pony" body

Neck
Medium length and carried well, slightly arched

Head
Neat and elegant, often displaying Appaloosa mottling around the muzzle

Coat
All different coat patterns, but always spotted

Legs
Short and well-made, in proportion

The POA should represent a Quarter Horse–Appaloosa cross in miniature, with the latter's striking coat patterns.

APPALOOSA

Native Americans were fiercely proud of their horses, and none more so than the Nez Perce tribe of the Pacific Northwest. Superb horsemen, the Nez Perce were perhaps the first to practice selective breeding, gelding inferior stallions and trading off poorer stock. Their striking spotted steeds were nicknamed "Palousey Horses"—for the Palouse River that runs through eastern Washington and northern Idaho—which quickly became Apalousey, then Appaloosa, the name being officially adopted in 1938. The Nez Perce lost most of their horses during the course of a war against U.S. Government forces in 1877, although they evaded capture with some 3,000 of them for almost four months. Those horses that survived were among the toughest and hardiest, as well as having the distinctive spotted coats. Western cattlemen were later to purchase the Nez Perce's surviving herds and continue their breeding.

THE FACTS	
Origin	Idaho, U.S.A.
Color	spotted, with 13 base colors and seven coat patterns
Height	14.2 hands (1.47 m)
Physique	varied, mottled skin, visible white sclera (ring around the eye), sparse mane and tail, striped hooves
Features	hardy, enduring
Temperament	easy-going, trainable
Use	riding, rodeo, ranching

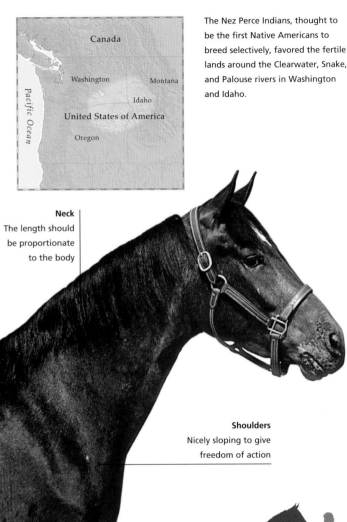

The Nez Perce Indians, thought to be the first Native Americans to breed selectively, favored the fertile lands around the Clearwater, Snake, and Palouse rivers in Washington and Idaho.

This mare is a true leopard spot—white with uniform-colored markings all over the body—but her foal has yet to develop its pattern.

Neck
The length should be proportionate to the body

Withers
Well-defined

Body
Compact and strong, proportionate and with well-sprung ribs

Shoulders
Nicely sloping to give freedom of action

Coat
This coat pattern is called blanket spot

Legs
Clean and slender

Feet
Small and hard, often striped—striped hooves are thought to be more resilient

Right, clockwise from top:
This herd of Appaloosas shows the varied coat and spot patterns seen in the breed.

The distinctive mottled muzzled and visible white sclera around the eye—sometimes called "human eye"—can clearly be seen on this handsome Appaloosa.

The Appaloosa was favored by the Native Americans and cowboys alike for its agility and "cow sense."

QUARTER HORSE

Its name does not, as some believe, allude to the amount of Thoroughbred blood in its breeding, but to the distance—a quarter of a mile—over which it was bred to race. Certainly, the Thoroughbred was to play a major role in the development of this lightning-fast sprinter. When put to native stock—chunky diminutive horses of Spanish descent, probably including some Arab, Turk, Barb, and Andalusian blood—the Thoroughbred produced tough, muscular horses possessed of explosive speed. Sprinters fell out of favor as distance racing became more popular in the nineteenth century, and the breed became diluted. But a horse called Steel Dust, foaled in 1843, was to have a lasting effect. His progeny, called Steel Dust Horses, were to become the modern Quarter Horses when the name was adopted in 1940, and today the breed numbers more than three million.

THE FACTS	
Origin	Virginia, U.S.A.
Color	all solid colors
Height	15.2 hands (1.57 m)
Physique	neat head, short, muscular neck, compact, short-coupled body, powerful hindquarters, strong hocks, fine legs, good feet
Features	agile, fast, easy to train
Temperament	intelligent, calm
Use	racing, riding, rodeo, ranching

The Quarter Horse is considered the oldest North American breed, originating in early seventeenth century Virginia. It is now most closely associated with the western states and is also very popular in Australia.

ANCESTRY

Thoroughbred blood put to native Spanish stock produced an agile, chunky sprinter with good looks, calm temperament, and impressive speed.

Iberian
Arabian
Thoroughbred
Morgan
Quarter Horse

The Arabian influence can be seen in the slightly concave profile of these Quarter Horses.

Quarters
Muscular with the impression of immense power

Body
Compact and chunky—the underline should be longer than the topline

Neck
Slightly arched, of medium length

Head
Attractive, short and neat

Shoulders
Nicely sloping to give freedom of action

Legs
Well-made, with hard joints

Feet
Small, well-formed, and sound

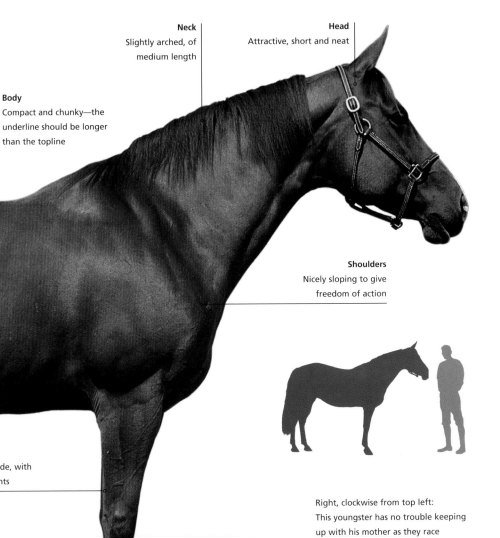

Right, clockwise from top left: This youngster has no trouble keeping up with his mother as they race through the surf in Oregon.

The Quarter Horse is capable of sprinting with explosive speed.

All coat colors are seen in the modern Quarter Horse.

SADDLEBRED

America's favorite riding horse is based on the now extinct Galloway and Hobby horses brought to the New World by early settlers. They were tough and active little horses and were natural pacers—moving the legs on the same side instead of diagonally, like a trotter. The offspring of these horses were called Narragansett Pacers after the Narragansett Bay area of Rhode Island. When the first Thoroughbreds arrived in the eighteenth century, they were crossed with the pacers to produce a horse with proud beauty and easy, elastic gaits. Wars were fought on the Saddlebred's back, and when the settlers travelled through the Cumberland Gap into what is now Kentucky, they did so on the Saddlebred, which became known as the Kentucky Saddler.

THE FACTS	
Origin	Kentucky and Rhode Island U.S.A.
Color	all solid colors, though predominantly chestnut
Height	16 hands (1.63 m)
Physique	small, attractive head, arched neck, high wither, sloping shoulder, deep chest, well-sprung ribs, long, slender legs
Features	athletic, gaited
Temperament	intelligent, spirited, kind
Use	riding, showing

The Saddlebred is based on the Narragansett Pacer, whose name comes from the Bay around Rhode Island. Crossed with Thoroughbreds, these horses were called Kentucky Saddlers after settlers moved west into that state.

ANCESTRY

The Saddlebred, based on the active little Galloway and Hobby horses, was bred as an all-purpose utility horse, with the pacers comfortable gaits.

Narragansett Pacer
Thoroughbred
Saddlebred

The Saddlebred is a horse of great beauty with considerable presence.

Neck
Long and carried high

Back
Sometimes rather long, level croup

Head
Elegant and refined

Shoulders
Have enough slope to allow characteristic free movement

Legs
Long and slender, lacking in bone below the knee

Feet
Well-shaped, trimmed long for the showring

These young Saddlebreds in Kentucky already show the elegance and elastic paces of the breed, which is predominantly chestnut in color.

STANDARDBRED

The Standardbred is so named because each and every one has to be able to trot a mile in under three minutes— the "standard time"—before they can be registered.

A Thoroughbred stallion called Messenger—foaled in 1780—is recognized as the founder of the breed, but it was his great-grandson, Hambletonian 10, who has a lasting legacy—all Standardbreds now can be traced back to him. Although the breed is renowned for its speed rather than its looks, Standardbreds retain some Thoroughbred characteristics, but are smaller and more muscular. The mile is still the standard distance for trotting races in America and mile-long tracks have been built. But trotting was the "racing for the people"—anyone could take part if they had a decent horse, and entire streets were closed off so races could take place. Many American towns today still has a "Race Street."

THE FACTS	
Origin	New England, U.S.A.
Color	all solid colors
Height	16 hands (1.57 m)
Physique	rather plain head, sometimes with a roman nose, medium-length neck, long back, muscular quarters, long, slender legs
Features	sound, agile, gaited
Temperament	intelligent, willing, calm
Use	trotting, pacing, riding

Messenger, the Standardbred's founding sire, stood at stud in Pennsylvania, New York, and New Jersey. He died on Long Island in 1808 at the age of 28. Hambletonian 10 was born in Sugar Loaf, New York.

ANCESTRY

The Thoroughbred Messenger is the founding sire of the Standardbred, and all of the modern breed can be traced back to his grandson, Hambletonian 10.

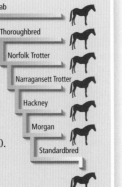

Arab
Thoroughbred
Norfolk Trotter
Narragansett Trotter
Hackney
Morgan
Standardbred

The Standardbred often shows Thoroughbred characteristics but has a somewhat plainer head.

Neck
Of medium-length, nicely set-on

Quarters
Muscular and very powerful

Back
Long but powerful, croup higher than the wither

Head
Rather plain, but still attractive, occasionally showing a Roman nose

Legs
Extremely sound and hard, with clean joints

Feet
Good and sound

Right, clockwise from top left:
A trotting race at Scarborough Downs, Maine.

Harness racing is big business—this horse, Ourasi, accumulated more than $2,900,000 winnings in his career.

Standardbred yearlings at Irvine Farm in Florida.

TENNESSEE WALKING HORSE

The first horse to be named for a state, this breed possesses a unique gait, the "running walk," which is both speedy and comfortable for the rider. The gait is inherited and cannot be taught. It is a square, four-beat gait with a gliding motion, and the horse bobs its head with each step—the running walk can be performed at up to 20 miles per hour (32 km/h). The horse credited with founding the breed was a black stallion called Allan, which had Morgan blood and also traced back to the Standardbred sire Hambletonian 10. Developed as a utility horse, the breed was intended for riding, driving, and light farm work. It was also popular on the southern plantations, whose owners needed a comfortable conveyance to inspect their properties—these horses became known as Plantation Walkers.

THE FACTS

Origin	Tennessee, U.S.A.
Color	all solid colors
Height	17 hands (1.73 m)
Physique	refined head, sloping shoulder, short-coupled, longer bottom line than topline to allow the long stride
Features	athletic, long stride, gaited
Temperament	affectionate, gentle, kind
Use	showing, riding

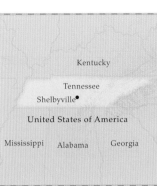

The breed was developed in the state of the same name in the nineteenth century. Each year, on the Sunday before Labor Day, the Tennessee Walking Horse National Show is held in Shelbyville, Tennessee.

ANCESTRY

Also known as Plantation Walker, the Tennessee Walker was developed for its supremely comfortable gaits, particularly its unique "running walk."

Narragansett Trotter/Pacer
Standardbred
Thoroughbred
Morgan
Saddlebred
Tennessee Walking Horse

The Tennessee Walker has the lean head of the Thoroughbred, whose influence in the breed came via Hambletonian 10.

Neck
Rather long, carried lower than that of the Standardbred or Saddlebred

Mane and tail
Usually left to grow long and flowing

Back
Rather short-coupled, deep through the girth

Head
Lean and handsome

Shoulders
Sloping

Legs
Long and slender, with powerful hindlegs

The Tennessee Walker is noted for its paces, and it is said "if you ride one today, you'll own one tomorrow."

RACKING HORSE

America's vast plantations are the spiritual home of this beautiful horse, whose good looks combine with the supremely comfortable "rack" or "single-foot" gait. The rack is a natural, inherited gait and is neither a trot nor a pace. It is sometimes called the single-foot because only one hoof strikes the ground at any one time. As it moves, its head remains still—unlike that of the Tennessee Walking Horse—its shoulders and quarters are very active, and it appears to "hop" from one foot to another. It was a boon to the plantation owners, as it could perform this gait for considerable lengths of time and was comfortable to ride. Its origins are undoubtedly with the Tennessee Walking Horse, which it closely resembles, but it was established as a separate breed in 1971 by a group of Alabama businessmen.

THE FACTS	
Origin	southern U.S.A.
Color	all colors, including spotted
Height	15.2 hands (1.57 m)
Physique	attractive head, long, elegant neck, sloping shoulder, powerful quarters, fine, long legs
Features	enduring, athletic, agile
Temperament	calm, kind, gentle
Use	showing, riding, harness

The Racking Horse was favored by the plantation owners of the American Deep South, who could tour their vast acreage in comfort on its back. It was recognized as a breed in 1971, registered at Decatur, Alabama.

Neck
Long and graceful

Body
Long back, with full flanks, rounded quarters

Head
Elegant and refined, carried high

Shoulders
Sloping and well-muscled

Tail
Full, luxurious and naturally raised

Legs
Long and fine, with muscular thighs and clean joints

Feet
Well-shaped and open, sound

The Racking Horse's gaits are inherited, not taught, and are extremely comfortable for the rider.

The Racking Horse is renowned for its beauty, elegance, stamina, and kind, affectionate temperament, as well as its glorious gaits.

ROCKY MOUNTAIN HORSE

Legend has it that a colt of striking coloring appeared in the foothills of the Appalacian Mountains in the 1880s. He was chocolate brown with flaxen mane and tail, but nothing was known about his breeding. Put to the Appalachian saddle mares, the colt produced a horse that was surefooted and comfortable, with a natural ambling four-beat gait. It became the mount of choice for postmen, doctors, and traveling preachers. The breed was used for plowing fields, herding cattle, traversing the area's steep and rugged trails, and driving the buggy to church on Sundays. A breeder named Sam Tuttle is credited with championing the Rocky Mountain Horse over the first three-quarters of the twentieth century. A great many Rocky Mountain Horses are descended from Tuttle's prize stallion, Old Tobe.

THE FACTS	
Origin	Kentucky, U.S.A.
Color	all solid color, no white permitted above the hock
Height	15 hands (1.52 m)
Physique	attractive head with bold eye and neat ears, medium-length neck, sloping shoulder, deep chest, powerful quarters, sound, slender legs, good feet
Features	long-lived, surefooted
Temperament	gentle, calm, intelligent
Use	showing, riding, endurance, competition

A breeder named Sam Tuttle of Spout Springs, Kentucky, is credited with maintaining and developing the Rocky Mountain Horse, which he used for rides through the Natural Bridge State Park in Powell County.

Neck
Medium length, elegant and slightly arched

Back
Long and well-muscled

Withers
Well-defined

Head
Attractive and refined

It is thought the original Rocky Mountain Horse, a colt of unknown lineage, was chocolate brown with flaxen mane and tail.

Chest
Wide and deep

Legs
Hard and clean, proportionate

Feet
Exceptionally sound

The Kentucky sunshine turns the coat of these Rocky Mountain Horses at Van Bert Farms, Stanton, to a burnished gold.

FLORIDA CRACKER

Whip-cracking Floridian cowboys gave this breed its name, although throughout its history it went by a variety of names—among them Chicksaw Pony, Seminole Pony, March Tackle, Grass Cut, Prairie Pony, and Florida Cow Pony. Like most American breeds, the Florida Cracker is Spanish in origin but, because of the state's isolation and continual trade with Cuba, those Spanish bloodlines were constantly refreshed. It is an attractive, agile little horse and, like many American breeds, has natural gaits that include the extremely comfortable amble. Changes in cattle herding practices almost spelled the end of the Florida Cracker, as it fell out of favor and was widely replaced by the bigger, stronger Quarter Horse. The breed was saved by a handful of ranching families who cherished these agile horses.

THE FACTS	
Origin	Florida U.S.A.
Color	all colors
Height	14.2 hands (1.47 m)
Physique	pretty head with straight or concave profile, fine, well-muscled neck, long, sloping shoulder, short, strong back, hard legs and feet
Features	agile, fast, strong
Temperament	intelligent, lively, genuine
Use	riding, ranching, Western riding

The breed takes its name from the Florida cowboys and their whips cracking loudly in the air. Because of Florida's comparative isolation, the Cracker is less diluted than some American breeds, retaining its Spanish heritage.

The Florida Cracker is small and agile, with many Spanish characteristics still apparent.

Croup
Sloping and short, with tail medium-set

Back
Short-coupled, underline is longer than the topline for power

Neck
Narrow with minimal crest, but well-defined

Withers
Pronounced but not too prominent

Head
Refined with straight or slightly concave profile

Shoulders
Sloping and well-muscled

Chest
Narrow to medium width

Movement
A distinctive single-foot gait called the "coon rack" is common

The Florida Cracker is tough and hardy, with surefooted, ground-covering gaits.

AZTECA

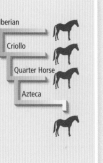

Mexico's "national horse" has replaced one of its founding breeds, the Criollo, in the country's affections, despite its relative youth. Until 1972, when the breed was founded, Mexico did not have an indigenous horse breed, and relied on other South American countries for its equine stock. The Mexican churros—or cowboys—wanted a horse that was fast, agile, and possessed innate "cow sense." So they put Andalusian stallions to their Quarter Horses and Criollo mares. The result, the Azteca, is perhaps one of the most notable equine success stories. It has the Andalusian's noble good looks, combined with the speed of the Quarter Horse and the almost balletic grace and agility of the Criollo. The first Azteca stallion was called Casarejo and was by the Andalusian Ocultado out of a Quarter Horse mare called Americana.

THE FACTS

Origin	Mexico
Color	all solid colors
Height	15 hands (1.52 m)
Physique	straight or slightly concave profile, expressive eyes, arched, muscular neck, defined wither, sloping shoulder, powerful quarters, excellent legs
Features	trainable, athletic, fast
Temperament	intelligent, obedient, sweet-natured
Use	riding, Western riding, bullfighting, competition

A relatively new breed, the Azteca is now considered the official national horse of Mexico, the country where it was developed. The Mexican Association of Breeders of Azteca Horses was established in 1982.

ANCESTRY

The modern ideal for the Azteca is not less than three-eighths nor more than five-eighths Andalusian or Quarter Horse blood, and no more than one-quarter Criollo.

Iberian
Criollo
Quarter Horse
Azteca

The courageous, athletic, and obedient Azteca is ideally suited to working with cattle, bullfighting, rodeo sports, dressage, and jumping.

Quarters
Powerful, with low- to medium-set tail

Withers
Defined, broad and muscled

Mane and tail
Long and flowing

Neck
Slightly arched with medium crest and broad base

Head
Noble and attractive, with wide forehead and expressive eyes

Legs
Strong and clean, with good bone

Feet
Very hard and sound

Mexico's national horse combines beauty and spirit, docility and grace, and is easy to train and comfortable to ride.

CRIOLLO

In 1535, Pedro de Mendoza sailed into the Rio de la Plata to found what was to become Buenos Aires. It is known that he took with him some 100 horses. Most of these did not survive the grueling journey, but those that did were the toughest and hardiest of stock. They were to form the basis of the Criollo. When Native Americans sacked Buenos Aires in 1540, many of the surviving Spanish horses and their offspring either escaped or were set free. Those horses bred in the wild, in fierce heat and extreme cold, with little water and only dry grass. Infusions of other blood have been introduced, with varying degrees of success, but the breed society is committed to producing only the best, pure-bred Criollo. It is no wonder the Criollo today, still just as hardy, is called "the King of the Pampas."

THE FACTS	
Origin	Argentina
Color	predominantly dun, but most colors occur
Height	14.2 hands (1.47 m)
Physique	straight or convex head, muscular neck, strong, sloping shoulder, broad, deep chest, compact back, powerful quarters, strong legs, hard feet
Features	hardy, long-lived, good doers
Temperament	willing, gentle, tractable
Use	riding, ranching, polo

Horses were brought to Argentina by Pedro de Mendoza, founder of Buenos Aires; they were undoubtedly of Spanish descent, probably a mix of Andalusian, Barb, and Sorraia. Those that survived had to be exceptionally tough.

ANCESTRY

Iberian influences are apparent in the Criollo, whose often seen dun coloring goes back to the Sorraia, as do the occasional primitive markings that occur.

Iberian
Lusitano
Dutch
Thoroughbred
Percheron
Criollo

All colors are seen in the Criollo, including broken-coated and spotted.

Quarters
Muscular and powerful

Back
Short and strong

Neck
Muscular and sturdy, prominent wither

Head
Distinctively convex in profile

Shoulders
Long and sloping, allowing for excellent action

Legs
Short and strong, with good bone, well-developed joints

Feet
Small and hard, very tough

Criollos in Argentina. A journey with two Criollos was made from Argentina to Washington D.C. by Professor Aime Tschiffely in 1925 to prove their endurance. The trip took two and a half years.

FALABELLA

In the 1840s, Irish settler Patrick Newell noticed tiny horses roaming free around Buenos Aires and he began to build a herd with the smallest he could find. He passed on the herd—and his breeding knowledge—to his son-in-law, Juan Falabella, who in turn shared it with his son Emilio, who passed it on to his son, Julio. They were to establish a breed of miniature horse—not a pony, despite its dimensions—using small Criollos, Appaloosas, and Pintos to ensure the gene pool did not get too limited. Shetland and Welsh Mountain ponies are also thought to have contributed. These horses, although they never grew in stature, gained a huge following. The Falabella is a true miniature horse, some as small as 28 inches (70 cm) high at the shoulder, and today is considered a rare breed, with only around 1,500 pure Falabellas registered with the official society and perhaps only a few thousand more worldwide.

THE FACTS	
Origin	Argentina
Color	all colors
Height	7.2 hands (0.76 m)
Physique	neat head, not too "ponyish," medium-length of neck, proportionate back and legs, small, boxy hooves, fine skin with silky hair
Features	hardy, tough
Temperament	sweet-natured, affectionate, gregarious
Use	pet, showing, harness

The Falabella family of Buenos Aires experimented with various bloodlines at their Recreo de Roca Ranch outside the capital to continue the line of tiny horses found roaming the Pampas by their forebear.

ANCESTRY

Small horses found in Argentina were thought either to be the result of adapting to the harsh environment or genetic mutation.

Iberian
Thoroughbred
Welsh
Shetland
Criollo
Falabella

Despite its stature, the Falabella is always considered to be a horse, not a pony.

Withers
Tends to flatness

Head
Should be more horsey than ponyish, but without undue heaviness

Shoulders
Rather upright, limiting movement; the breed is not suitable for riding

Legs
Should be proportionate

Feet
Small and neat, can sometimes be boxy with short cannon bones.

Right, clockwise from top left:
The Falabella is highly prized as a pet due to its tiny size and sweet nature.

Two Falabella fillies at play; the breed is affectionate and they love children.

All colors are seen in the Falabella, including blue eyes and attractively marked skewbalds and piebalds.

MANGALARGA MARCHADOR

Its mellifluous name suits this enchanting breed so well, although perhaps not as well as that of its founding sire, Sublime. Thought to be an Alter-Real, Sublime was presented in 1812 to Gabriel Francisco Junqueira, Baron of Alfenas. The baron put his new stallion to Spanish Jennet and North African Barb mares—the resulting offspring were called Sublime Horses. Elegant and good-looking, these horses possessed a cadenced, rhythmic gait called the "marcha." When some were purchased by the Hacienda Mangalarga, the Mangalarga Marchador was born. The breed has three distinct paces—the marcha picada, a similar pace to the Icelandic Horse's tolt; the marcha batida, a diagonal gait similar to the "fox-trot;" and center march, similar to the Tennessee Walking Horse's running walk.

THE FACTS

Origin	Brazil
Color	bay, chestnut, roan, gray, dun
Height	16 hands (1.63 m)
Physique	quality head, elegant, muscular neck, medium-length back, powerful quarters, low-set tail, long, slender legs, sound feet
Features	elegant, gaited
Temperament	lively, willing, intelligent
Use	riding, harness

The breed was developed by the Baron of Alfenas at his Hacienda Campo Alegre in the state of Minas Gerais. The breed association, now called the Associação Brasileira dos Criadores do Cavalo Mangalarga Marchador, has some 190,000 registered horses.

ANCESTRY

The name comes from the Hacienda Mangalarga, which purchased Sublime Horses from their breeder, and from the breed's distinctive gaits.

Alter-Real
Spanish Jennet
Barb
Mangalarga Marchador

Elegant and good-looking, these horses possessed a cadenced, rhythmic gait called the "marcha."

Quarters
Short and powerful, tail set low

Back
Medium in length and well-muscled

Neck
Arched and muscular, carried high and proudly

Head
Refined with a straight profile and Barb-like in appearance

Legs
Long and slender, but sound

Feet
Hard and sound

The Mangalarga Marchador is famed for its good looks and elegance as much as the flowing paces that gave it its name.

MISSOURI FOX-TROTTER

It is no coincidence that this breed is named for a dance. The horse, developed in the Missouri Ozarks, has a gentle demeanor and a signature gait—the four-beat, fluid fox-trot. Smooth and comfortable, no special shoeing is required for the horse to perform the fox-trot, in which it walks with its front feet and trots with its hind. There is no jarring for the rider and little fatigue for the horse, which can keep up the fox-trot for long periods. It is supremely adept at covering the mountainous region of its homeland. When pioneers spread across the Mississippi River from Tennessee and Virginia, they brought their horses with them. The Fox-Trotter, originally known as the Ozark Hill Horse, was the must-have utility horse for the Ozark cattle farmers, even after mechanization. The breed registry was opened in Ava, Missouri, in 1948, and closed in 1983.

THE FACTS	
Origin	Missouri, U.S.A.
Color	most solid colors
Height	15 hands (1.52 m)
Physique	fine head, sloped shoulder, short, strong back, well-muscled legs, good feet
Features	surefooted, agile
Temperament	gentle, calm
Use	Western riding, show

The breed association for the Fox-Trotter was opened in Ava, Missouri, in 1958. In 2002, the Missouri Fox-Trotter was adopted as the official state horse.

ANCESTRY

Settlers from Kentucky, Tennessee, and Virginia brought their own horses into Missouri, probably a mix of Arab, Morgans, and Tennessee Walkers.

Morgan
Arab
Saddlebred
Standardbred
Tennessee Walking Horse
Missouri Fox-Trotter

The Fox-Trotter is widely recognized as a horse for all seasons and situations, from ranching to appearances in movies.

Mane
Of proportionate length, well set-on

Body
Short, strong back, deep body, well-sprung ribs

Head
Elegant and refined

Shoulders
Long and sloping

Legs
Muscular and tapered

Feet
Strong and well-made

The Missouri Fox-Trotter is renowned for its beauty and gentle temperament as well as its stamina, surefootedness, and ground-covering gaits.

PASO FINO

"Los Caballo de Paso Fino" translates literally as "the horse with the fine walk," and this glorious equine is aptly named. Its Spanish heritage is apparent in its presence and noble bearing, and its natural gait, usually exhibited from birth. It wasn't until the Second World War, when American servicemen were stationed in Puerto Rico, that the Paso Fino's fame spread outside Latin America. Paso Fino Horses were exported from Puerto Rico and, later, Columbia to the United States. The horse's gait is performed at three speeds—the Classic Fino, with rapid footfall and short steps and extension; Paso Corto, moderate speed, with ground-covering but unhurried steps; and Paso Largo, the fastest speed, with longer stride and extension. All are very smooth and comfortable for the rider.

THE FACTS

Origin	South America and Caribbean
Color	most solid colors
Height	14 hands (1.42 m)
Physique	refined head with straight profile, arched neck carried high, defined wither, sloping shoulder, strong back, longer topline than bottom line, fine legs with good joints
Features	agile, athletic, strong
Temperament	spirited, willing, gentle
Use	riding, harness, competition, show

The Paso Fino flourished in Puerto Rico and Columbia—where it was known as the Paso Columbiano—and later other Latin American countries, such as Cuba, the Dominican Republic, and Venezuela.

ANCESTRY

The Paso Fino's Spanish heritage is apparent in its proud bearing and elegant good looks; it is closely related to the Peruvian Paso.

Andalusian
Barb
Spanish Jennet
Paso Fino

Neck
Muscular and nicely arched

Quarters
Powerful and well-muscled

Back
Longer topline than underline

Head
Noble, well-shaped, sometimes slightly convex

Shoulders
Long and sloping

Chest
Muscular and deep

Legs
Clean with good joints

Feet
Hard and sound

The Paso Fino has the fine, sculpted head of its Iberian forebears.

Clockwise from left:
The Paso Fino has three separate four-beat gaits, the Paso Fino, the Corto, and the Largo, a fast, extended, ground-swallowing gait.

The Spanish origins, particularly the Andalusian, are apparent in this fine horse.

The noble profile and bold eye is typical of the Paso Fino.

These youngsters already exhibit the breed's natural lively inquisitiveness.

PERUVIAN PASO

Great Peruvians are born, not made, so the saying goes. The natural gait of the Peruvian Paso is highly prized and no horses in the showring may be shod, nor have hooves longer than 4 inches (10 cm). The Paso's four-beat gait has neither the vertical movement of the trot nor the lateral motion of the pace—the sensation is more of a side-to-side rock. The breed also exhibits what is known as "termino," in which the foreleg rolls outward in a graceful motion—much like the arms of a swimmer in front crawl—before it strikes the ground. The horse's other characteristic is "brio," that hard-to-define "look at me" quality that makes it a natural showman, performing with a enchanting mixture of arrogance and exuberance. It is also kind and tractable, the perfect equine partner. Although the Paso Fino is closely related, its Peruvian cousin is accepted as a separate breed.

THE FACTS	
Origin	Peru
Color	all solid colors
Height	14.2 hands (1.47 m)
Physique	straight or concave profile, crested neck, short back, strong quarters, angled hocks, abundant mane and tail
Features	agile, proud, a natural showman
Temperament	eager to please, spirited
Use	riding, Western riding, harness, show

Peru's national horse is the product of selective breeding for centuries to retain the Paso's unique gaits and undeniable beauty—no outside blood has been introduced.

Neck
Short and upright, but well-muscled

Back
Short-coupled, muscular

Head
Straight profile

These Peruvian Pasos show the natural balance and graceful movement of the breed.

Legs
Set on to allow for the "termino," a sweeping motion unique to the breed

Feet
Strong and sound

Clockwise from above:
The Peruvian Paso is highly prized in its
native land and there is a national show
held at Lima to celebrate the breed.

The Peruvian Paso has a quality known as
"brio"—the "look at me" arrogance of
the natural showman.

It is said that the Peruvian Paso's gaits
are so smooth a rider could carry a glass
of water without spilling a drop.

CAMPOLINA

A black mare called Medéia is credited as the matriarch of this Brazilian breed, which was started by Cassiano Antonio de Silva Campolina at his stud, Fazenda Tanque, in 1857. But it was Medéia's son, a stunning iron-gray colt called Monarca, who was to be the breed's founding sire. He was the result of breeding Medéia to a pure-bred Andalusian, and stood as a stallion for 25 years. Cassiano Campolina experimented with several stallions, put mainly to Criollo mares, in his quest to establish a breed with good looks, presence, and smooth, comfortable gaits. He used a part-bred Clydesdale called Golias; a Holstein named Teffer; Yanke Prince, a Saddlebred; and Rio Verde, a Mangalarga Marchador. This last gave the Campolina its gaits, among them the Marcha Verdedair—the True March—at which it can maintain speeds of 6 to 8 miles per hour (10–13 km/h).

THE FACTS	
Origin	Brazil
Color	all solid colors
Height	16 hands (1.63 m)
Physique	slightly convex profile, crested neck, good shoulders, compact body, hard legs and excellent feet
Features	gaited, agile, enduring
Temperament	intelligent, kind
Use	riding, harness

The breed is named for its founder Cassiano Campolina, who developed it at his ranch at Entre Rios de Minas in Brazil. Campolina experimented with several stallions, put mainly to Criollo mares, in his quest to establish a breed with good looks, presence, and smooth, comfortable gaits.

ANCESTRY

Andalusian and Criollo stock were to form the basis of this breed, but Clydesdale and Holstein blood has also played a part.

Andalusian
Barb
Clydesdale
Holstein
Saddlebred
Mangalarga Marchador
Campolina

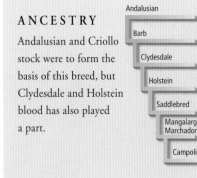

The Campolina has inherited gaits from the Mangalarga Marchador.

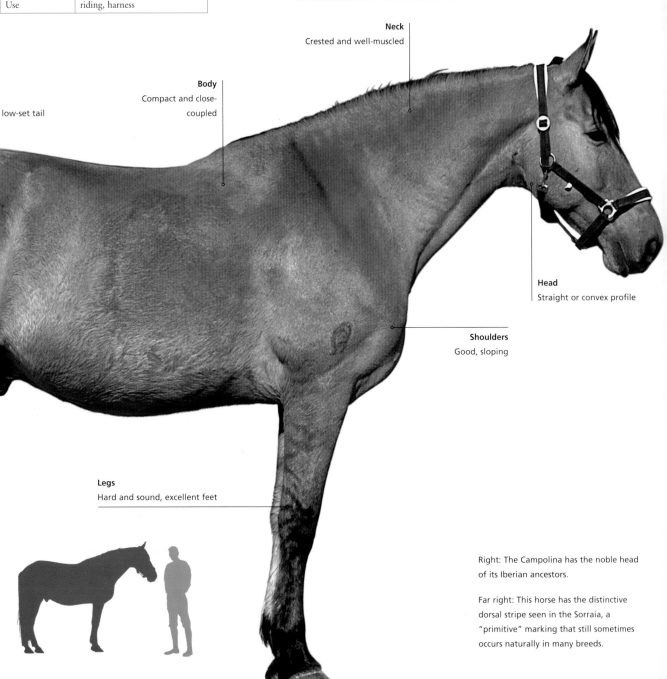

Neck
Crested and well-muscled

Body
Compact and close-coupled

Croup
Sloping, low-set tail

Head
Straight or convex profile

Shoulders
Good, sloping

Legs
Hard and sound, excellent feet

Right: The Campolina has the noble head of its Iberian ancestors.

Far right: This horse has the distinctive dorsal stripe seen in the Sorraia, a "primitive" marking that still sometimes occurs naturally in many breeds.

CONNEMARA

Wild ponies have existed in north-west Ireland for thousands of years and are probably descended from the now-extinct Celtic Pony. Legend has it that these ponies bred with shipwrecked Spanish horses, and whatever the truth of this, they almost certainly have Spanish Jennet blood, as well as Arab and Barb. Their natural environment was wild and harsh, and the ponies developed an innate surefootedness—one misstep could send them crashing to their deaths. They became tough and hardy, surviving on meager rations. The breed has been influenced by Thoroughbred, Hackney, and Welsh blood. An important stallion called Cannonball, of Welsh and Connemara blood, became the first to be entered into the studbook in 1926—the breed society was founded in 1923.

THE FACTS

Origin	Ireland
Color	predominantly gray, dun, bay, brown
Height	14 hands (1.42 m)
Physique	neat, pretty pony head, medium length, arched neck, good sloping shoulders, broad, deep chest, compact body, excellent legs and feet
Features	tough, hardy, athletic
Temperament	intelligent, kind, honest
Use	riding, hunting, competition

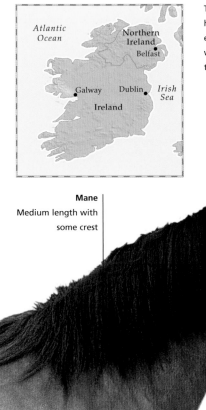

The rocky coast of western Ireland has a savage beauty, and is a harsh environment for its native ponies, which had to be tough and resilient to survive the conditions.

ANCESTRY

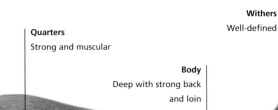

The Connemara is the result of Iberian stock being crossed with the now extinct Celtic Pony, although how the Spanish horses came to Ireland is open to debate.

Celtic Pony
Spanish Jennet
Arab
Barb
Thoroughbred
Hackney
Welsh
Connemara

Quarters
Strong and muscular

Body
Deep with strong back and loin

Withers
Well-defined

Mane
Medium length with some crest

Head
Attractive, medium-length pony head well set-on to neck

Shoulders
Quality and nicely sloping for free paces

Legs
Good bone, well-shaped joints, low-set hocks, muscular

The hardy Connemara makes a superb all-round sports pony for children and adults alike.

Renowned for its hardiness, it was feared this vital characteristic would be lost as owners stabled their horses, so in the 1920s small herds of Connemara were turned loose to live wild.

DALES

A Friesian in miniature, the proof that England's Dales Pony descended from the European breed is in its very outline. The Dales is a tough little horse, with great strength and stamina, and an iron constitution. It probably descended from the now extinct Pennine Pony, which would have been crossed with the heavy Friesian breed during the Roman occupation. Later, infusions of Scottish Galloway blood lightened the pony and gave it speed and surefootedness. Further blood included that of Clydesdale, Norfolk Trotter, and Yorkshire Coach Horse, plus the Welsh Cob stallion, Comet, who was introduced in the late 1800s to improve the breed's gait. Originally used as a pack animal to carry heavy loads of lead across the Pennines, today the Dales is a popular children's pony, with a charming nature to match its good looks. As it can carry an adult, and has innate jumping ability, it can lay claim to the title "true all-rounder."

THE FACTS

Origin	Pennines, northern England
Color	black, brown, bay, gray, roan
Height	14.2 hands (1.47 m)
Physique	neat pony head with no dishing, strong neck, long, sloping shoulders, deep chest, short-coupled, excellent legs with plenty of bone, hard feet, abundant mane and tail
Features	strong, surefooted
Temperament	kind, intelligent, gentle
Use	riding, harness

This breed is named for the Yorkshire Dales—an upland region of valleys, hills and moors that spans a large part of Yorkshire and part of neighboring Cumbria. Most of the area now falls within the Yorkshire Dales National Park.

Head
Neat and pony-like, with a broad forehead

ANCESTRY

Trotting races were very popular in England during the eighteenth and nineteenth centuries, and both Norfolk and Yorkshire blood was introduced to the Dales to improve its trotting ability and speed.

Friesian
Scottish Galloway
Clydesdale
Norfolk Trotter
Yorkshire Roadster
Welsh Cob
Dales

Quarters
Deep and long, powerful

Body
Short-coupled with well-sprung ribs

Neck
Long and slightly arching, stallions have a good crest

Chest
Deep, with plenty of heart-room

Although Dales Ponies are predominantly black or gray, roan examples are sometimes seen.

Legs
Short and muscular, with excellent joints and flat, flinty bone, plenty of silky feather

The Dales is an easy keeper, able to thrive on meager rations, and is renowned for the quality and soundness of its excellent legs and feet.

Feet
Hard and sound, open at the heels

FELL

Like its close cousin, the Dales, the Fell was based on the extinct Pennine Pony, which was dark in color and stood little more than 13 hands (1.32 m). The Pennine Pony probably lived in the north of England for millennia, and it was only when the Romans came, bringing with them their war horses, that fresh blood was introduced. This new blood produced a larger, stronger pony, big enough for a man to ride. The Vikings used these ponies to plow and pull sledges, the Normans for shepherding. By the thirteenth century there was a brisk wool trade, so the ponies were used to transport merchandise across the country, using the old trails still extant today. Although the Fell is predominantly black, other colors are sometimes seen.

THE FACTS	
Origin	Lake District, England
Color	black, brown, bay, gray
Height	14 hands (1.42 m)
Physique	chiseled pony head, medium length neck with moderate crest on stallions, well laid-back, sloping shoulders, long shoulder blade, short, strong back, excellent legs and feet, some feather
Features	hardy, alert, tough
Temperament	lively, sweet-natured
Use	riding, harness

Horse trails criss-cross northern England and were used for centuries for transporting goods across the Pennines, a low mountain range that separates northwest England from the northeast.

ANCESTRY

Friesian blood was added to the old Pennine Pony during the Roman occupation of Britain (A.D. 43–410). This would have added height and substance.

Friesian

Iberian

Galloway

Fell

A small white star, as seen on this handsome foal, is acceptable, but excessive white markings are discouraged within the breed.

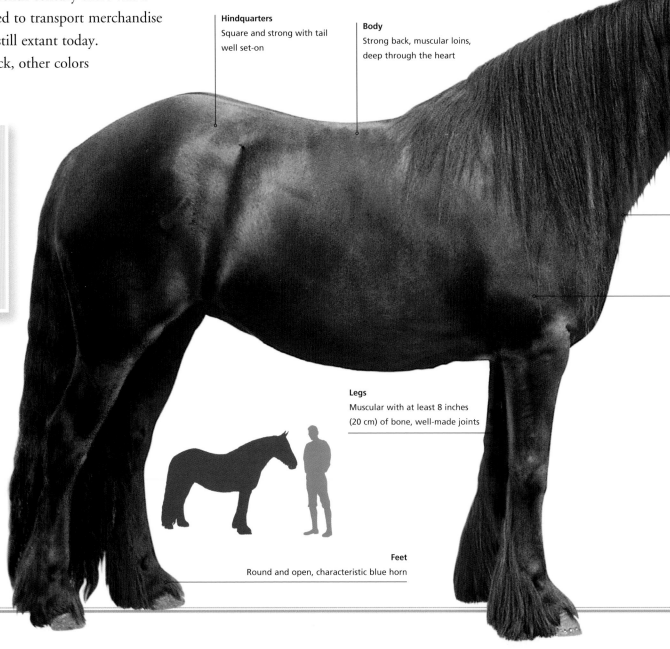

Head
Fine and chiselled, nicely tapering to muzzle

Hindquarters
Square and strong with tail well set-on

Body
Strong back, muscular loins, deep through the heart

Neck
Good length of rein, well-made but not too heavy

Shoulders
Sloping with a good, long shoulderblade, nicely muscled

Legs
Muscular with at least 8 inches (20 cm) of bone, well-made joints

Feet
Round and open, characteristic blue horn

Right: The Fell Pony, like the Dales, is famed for its exceptional paces, with a long-striding walk, well-balanced trot, and smooth and free canter.

Inset: While it makes a superb all-round riding pony, the Fell is also excellent in harness. The Duke of Edinburgh, husband of Britain's Queen Elizabeth II, drove a team of Fell Ponies before he retired from competition.

DARTMOOR

Named for the region of southwest England from where it originates, the Dartmoor is a true mountain and moorland pony, supremely adapted to its environment. It is known that small ponies existed in the region at least since the Middle Ages. One of the earliest recorded references to these ponies is in the will of a Saxon Bishop, Alfwold of Crediton, who died in 1012. When tin mining was the main industry in the southwest, the Dartmoor was used as a pack pony; when the mines closed, many ponies were turned loose on to the moor. It is only comparatively recently that efforts have been made to retain and maintain the true pure-bred Dartmoor Pony. Sweet natured, attractive, and easy to keep, they make superb companions and children's mounts.

THE FACTS

Origin	southwest England
Color	bay, brown, black, gray, chestnut, roan
Height	12.2 hands (1.27 m)
Physique	small head with large, kindly eye, medium length neck, good, sloping shoulder, strong back, good depth of girth and plenty of heart room, strong legs, excellent feet
Features	sturdy, tough, active
Temperament	kind, intelligent, gentle
Use	riding, harness

ANCESTRY

Arab and Welsh lines have been used to refine and develop the Dartmoor, which suffered from a disastrous infusion of Shetland blood in the early nineteenth century.

Native stock
Thoroughbred
Arab
Welsh Mountain
Fell
Dartmoor

Dartmoor, in the southwest of England, is one of the country's national parks, and is a wild place of granite upland capped with exposed hilltops called tors—its native pony had to have a tough constitution.

Head
Small and pretty with neat ears and large kindly eye

Quarters
Muscular and in proportion, tail well set-on

Body
Well ribbed-up with plenty of heart room

Neck
Of medium length, stallions should have a moderate crest

Shoulders
Laid back and sloping, not too fine at the wither

Most solid colors are seen in the Dartmoor, but piebalds and skewbalds are not permitted in the breed.

Legs
All should have plenty of bone, plenty of length from hip to hock

Feet
Hard and well-shaped

Dartmoor Ponies grazing in the wilds of the national park that is their natural home, dotted with heathers and granite tors.

EXMOOR

Living in one of the harshest environments in England, the Exmoor Pony has adapted supremely to its surroundings. There is little shelter on the moor, and temperatures can plummet well below freezing. The Exmoor has several unique features to protect against the elements, including the "toad eye," a heavy upper brow to shield the eyes from the wind and rain. It also has a "snow chute" or "ice tail," a growth of short, coarse hairs at the top of the tail to channel snow and rain away from its body. In the winter, it grows a double-layered coat, which provides both insulation and waterproofing. Hardy and strong, the little Exmoor can carry an adult with ease, but its sweet temper also makes it a highly suitable child's pony. It is adaptable and brave, quick to learn and eager to please, and has a cat-like jumping ability.

THE FACTS

Origin	southwest England
Color	brown with black points and "mealy" muzzle
Height	12.3 hands (1.3 m)
Physique	small head with broad forehead and bold eye, compact body, well-sprung ribs, short, clean legs with good bone, hard, well-made feet
Features	hardy, agile, strong
Temperament	gentle, kind, friendly
Use	racing, endurance, competition

The home of the Exmoor Pony was formerly a royal forest and hunting ground. It is now protected as a national park. Today, ponies still run wild on the moor.

ANCESTRY

The Exmoor displays the mealy markings and primitive markings that betray its ancient ancestry—it is thought to be one of most pure of Britain's native breeds.

Przewalski's Horse
Tarpan
Exmoor

The Exmoor Pony is supremely adapted to endure the harsh moorland winters.

Head
Has the "primitive" mealy muzzle and distinctive "toad eye"

Body
Compact and strong, with well-sprung ribs

Neck
Medium length of rein, nicely muscled

Legs
Clean and hard, plenty of bone and well-developed joints

Feet
Neat, hard, and well-shaped

Top right: The stunningly beautiful Exmoor National Park, home to its eponymous ponies, spans the counties of Devon and Somerset.

Right: Youngstock on the ancient moor—the Exmoor is recognized as endangered by the British Rare Breeds Survival Trust.

NEW FOREST

Elegant, sweet natured, and eager to please, the New Forest Pony has lived in the woodland for which it was named since at least 1016 when grazing rights to the New Forest, a royal hunting ground, were granted to commoners. The New Forest is not a feral breed—to this day the ponies have owners who pay an annual fee for commoners' grazing rights. Other breeds have been introduced to improve the stock, including Arab, Thoroughbred, Welsh, and Hackney. Additionally, a polo pony called Field Marshall stood at stud in the forest from 1918 to 1919 and had a significant influence. Some other native blood has been introduced in small quantities to ensure the breed retains its "pony" quality. The New Forest Pony studbook was opened in 1906.

THE FACTS	
Origin	southern England
Color	all solid colors, except blue-eyed cream
Height	14.2 hands (1.47 m)
Physique	attractive head, sloping shoulders, long back, narrow rib cage, strong quarters, long, slender legs, hard feet
Features	agile, tough, versatile
Temperament	calm, intelligent, gentle
Use	riding, harness, competition, ideal child's pony

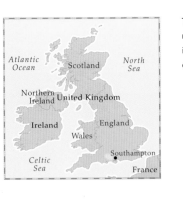

The New Forest includes the largest remaining unenclosed pasture land in the crowded southeastern corner of England.

ANCESTRY

While Arab, Thoroughbred, Welsh, and Hackney blood has been used to improve the New Forest, it has been pure-bred for the past 50 years.

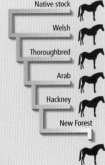

Native stock
Welsh
Thoroughbred
Arab
Hackney
New Forest

Body
Well-sprung ribs and plenty of heart room, but not broad across the back

Head
Neat and pretty, very "pony" in character

Neck
Medium length, nicely muscled with some arch

Shoulders
Sloping

Legs
Long and slender, but well-made and strong with plenty of flat bone

Feet
Hard and round

The Arab and Thoroughbred influence can be seen in this New Forest's refined head, although it retains its pony character.

Sweet tempered and versatile, the New Forest makes an ideal family pony and all-rounder, capable of carrying an adult and narrow enough to suit a child.

ERISKAY

A rare breed, the Eriskay is thought to be the last surviving descendant of the now extinct Celtic Pony that inhabited much of the northern British Isles. Small ponies of similar type can be seen on carvings by the Pict people, who inhabited the area during the Dark Ages. It takes its name from Eriskay—or Eric's Isle—in Scotland's Outer Hebrides. They were used by crofters—smallholding farmers in the Scottish Highlands and Western Isles—for hauling peat and seaweed, working the land, and even taking the children to school. In such isolated, harsh conditions, the ponies had to be tough and able to survive on poor forage. The Eriskay was almost wiped out due to cross-breeding and today is considered to be endangered with only around 420 left in the world.

THE FACTS	
Origin	Outer Hebrides
Color	predominantly gray, black, brown
Height	13.2 hands (1.37 m)
Physique	largish head, well-muscled neck and shoulders, deep chest, strong back, fine legs with a little feather, small and upright feet
Features	hardy, good doers
Temperament	placid, amenable, intelligent
Use	riding, harness, ideal family pony

Modern Eriskay Ponies are the last surviving remnants of the original native ponies of the Western Isles of Scotland.

Head
Rather large, with broad forehead, deep jaw and tapering muzzle

Body
Long rib cage and short loin, sloping croup

Eriskay Ponies are predominantly gray, although this charming foal appears to have the "primitive" dun coloring.

Neck
Strong and well-muscled, good length of rein

Chest
Deep without being too broad

Legs
Proportionate to the body, flat bone, fine feather

Feet
Small and neat with hard horn, somewhat upright

Well adapted to cope with the harsh, wet, and windy climate of the Scottish islands, as well as having to survive on meager food supplies, Eriskays have evolved into tough and hardy animals.

HIGHLAND

Since at least the eighth century B.C., ponies have roamed the harsh and remote Scottish Highlands and Western Isles. The ancient roots of the Highland Pony can be seen in its color and markings. Highlands are often dun, or variations of dun, with the "primitive" dorsal stripe along the back, black points, and zebra stripes on the legs and sometimes the shoulders. The Highland is the only native British breed that continues to exhibit these characteristics without specific breeding selection. Used for centuries as crofters' pack ponies, the Highland is still popular as its innate surefootedness and rugged toughness make it ideal for transporting heavy loads across the landscape. It also makes a perfect family pony, as it is docile and gentle, as well as being strong and agile.

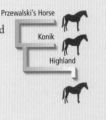

THE FACTS

Origin	western Scotland
Color	all shades of dun, gray, black, bay
Height	14.2 hands (1.47 m)
Physique	fine, sculpted head, powerful neck, good shoulders, well-proportioned body, strong quarters, excellent legs with plenty of bone, good feet
Features	hardy, sure-footed, agile
Temperament	docile, gentle, intelligent
Use	riding, hunting, harness, stalking, competition, all-rounder

Ponies have existed in the north of Scotland and its islands for centuries, and have adapted supremely to the harsh conditions—the Highland grows a thick, badger-like coat in the winter for protection against the elements.

ANCESTRY

The Highland's zebra markings, dorsal stripe, and dun coloring—with all its variations—illustrate its links to the ancient Konik and Przewalski's Horse.

Przewalski's Horse

Konik

Highland

Quarters
Powerful and pleasingly muscled

Body
Proportionate and compact, with well-sprung ribs

Head
Alert with a kindly eye, broad-muzzled and deep-jowled

Neck
Good length of rein

Shoulders
Well-placed and sloping

Chest
Plenty of room for heart and lungs

Legs
Hard, flat bone, broad knee joints and short cannon bones, some silky feather

Feet
Well-shaped dark horn

A playful Highland Pony foal. The breed is an easy keeper, economical to feed and hardy enough to live outside.

Gordon Muir, stalker and gamekeeper at Glen Batrick Lodge on Jura in Scotland's Inner Hebrides, leads a young guest along the shore of Loch Tarbert on a Highland Pony.

SHETLAND

Said to be the most ancient native pony breed in Great Britain, the Shetland Pony has been shaped by the remote islands from which it takes its name. Excavations on the islands have discovered bones of small ponies that lived during the Bronze Age. Domesticated by the islanders, the ponies became indispensable. Despite their tiny stature, they are immensely strong and capable of carrying an adult. They were used to carry peat from the bogs, which was used as fuel, and seaweed for fertilizing crops. Because of the islands' isolation, the Shetland breed has been kept remarkably pure, and its strength and durability are legendary. No place on Shetland is more than 4 miles (6 km) from the sea, and in the harshest of winters, when forage was poor, the ponies would move to the shore to graze on seaweed. Larger animals would not be able to survive in these conditions; the smaller ponies had the advantage.

THE FACTS	
Origin	Shetland Isles, northern Scotland
Color	any color, except spotted
Height	10.2 hands (1.07 m)
Physique	small head with neat ears and a bold eye, well-defined wither, sloping shoulder, well-sprung ribs, broad quarters, strong legs, hard, well-shaped feet
Features	strong, hardy, enduring
Temperament	gentle, calm, brave
Use	riding, harness

There have been ponies on the remote Shetland isles for millennia, and the Shetland has evolved with relatively few outcrosses because of the difficulties of transporting horses to the islands by sea.

Head
Small and pretty, with neat, erect ears and broad forehead

Body
Strong and well-muscled

Neck
In proportion and properly set-on

Shoulders
Must be sloping, not upright, from well-defined wither

Right, clockwise from top left:
A Shetland mare and her charming foal, Somerset, England.

Fast and furious action from the ultra-competitive Shetland Pony Grand National held at the London International Horse Show, Olympia.

The characteristic neat, pretty head of a Shetland.

Inquisitive young ponies grazing on the Shetland Isles.

The Shetland is hardy enough to survive the long, dark, and cold winters of its island home.

Legs
Balanced and well-made, with flat bone and strong joints

Feet
Small, round, and very tough

WELSH SECTION A AND B

The Welsh Mountain Pony's Arabian ancestry is apparent in its pretty, dished head. The attractive, hardy little ponies that inhabited the Welsh mountains were—and still are—highly popular. It is said that Julius Caeser established a stud at Bala Lake, and it was the Romans who introduced Arab blood to the indigenous stock. The oldest and smallest of the four Welsh breeds, the Mountain Pony—or Section A—has been used as the foundation for the other three. The modern pony is found the world over, and loved as much for its happy personality as its good looks and hardiness. The Welsh Pony—Section B in the studbook—has all the Mountain Pony qualities, but is slightly bigger and finer and makes an excellent riding pony with a low, smooth action.

THE FACTS	
Origin	Wales
Color	all solid colors
Height	Section A: 12 hands (1.22 m) Section B: 13.2 hands (1.37 m)
Physique	pretty head, with pronounced dishing (Section A), long neck (Section B), sloping shoulders, compact body, slender legs, good feet
Features	tough, agile, fast
Temperament	gentle, kind, spirited
Use	riding, competition, harness

Ponies have been been bred in the mountains of Wales for centuries, and have proved the theory of "survival of the fittest," with sound constitution, iron-hard limbs and natural intelligence.

ANCESTRY

The Welsh Mountain Pony, Section A of the studbook, is the "prototype" of the other three Sections.

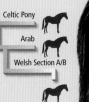

Celtic Pony

Arab

Welsh Section A/B

Body
Strong and deep, plenty of room through the girth

Head
Very pretty, with a pronounced dished or concave profile, particularly in the Section A

Neck
Long and lean, some crest on stallions, pronounced wither

The Arab ancestry can clearly be seen in this Welsh Mountain Pony's beautiful head.

Legs
Well-set, with good bone, flat, straight hocks

Action
Quick, free and straight from the shoulder, knees and hocks well-flexed with powerful leverage well under the body

Section A
Mountain Pony

Section B
Welsh Pony

Clockwise from top left:
A palomino Section A stallion enjoying his freedom in Texas—the Welsh breeds are extremely popular in America.

The refined head of the Welsh Section B, slightly bigger than the Mountain Pony.

Despite his shaggy winter coat, the quality of this Section B stallion shines through.

A Section A mare and her foal

WELSH SECTION C AND D

Andalusian blood played a role in forming the Welsh Pony of Cob Type (Section C in the studbook) and its influence can be seen in its noble head. Norfolk Trotter, Pembroke Carthorse, and Hackney blood have also been introduced. Originally known as the Powys Horse, the Welsh Section C, answered the call for a bigger, stronger pony that was an easy keeper and had all the pony qualities, but could be used to draw loads of timber, work the upland farms, and pull the family cart. The Welsh Cob (Section D) is larger still—indeed, there is no upper height limit in the studbook—and is said to be the best ride and drive pony in the world. Norfolk Trotter and Yorkshire Coach Horse blood were introduced to increase height and action. Trotting Comet, as his name suggests, a trotter, and True Briton, by a Yorkshire Coach Horse out of an Arab mare, both played a major role in the Cob's development.

THE FACTS	
Origin	Wales
Color	all solid colors
Height	Section C: 13.2 hands (1.37 m) Section D: 15 hands (1.52 m)
Physique	quality pony head, long neck, strong, laid-back shoulders, powerful, long quarters, long legs with some fine feather, hard, dense feet
Features	hardy, active, strong
Temperament	lively, trainable, amenable
Use	riding, harness, competition

The hill farmers of Wales discovered they needed a bigger, stronger animal to work their land, but something not as heavy as a draft horse, which would struggle in the terrain.

Head
Full of quality and retaining pony character

Back
Nicely coupled and strong with well-sprung ribs and plenty of heart room

Quarters
Long and powerful

Neck
Of good length and well-carried

Shoulders
Well laid-back and strong

ANCESTRY

It is said the Welsh Cob should look, in silhouette, like a scaled-up version of the Section A. Trotter blood was used to increase the height of the Section C and D.

Welsh Section A
Pembroke Carthorse
Andalusian
Yorkshire Coach Horse
Norfolk Trotte
Hackney
Welsh Section C/D

Andalusian influence can be seen in the head of this Welsh Section C, with the broadness of the forehead and the bold eye.

Section C
Cob Type

Section D
Welsh Cob

Feet
Well-shaped with dense, hard hoofs

Legs
Plenty of bone below the well-developed knee, clean hocks

Right, clockwise from top left:
The Welsh Section D's glorious action makes it a popular competition pony, ridden as well as in harness.

This Cob has his eye on the photographer—all Welsh breeds are said to be natural showmen.

A Welsh Section C mare and foal— the gray coloring comes from Arabian and Andalusian ancestors.

AUSTRALIAN STOCK HORSE

Horses arrived in Australia along with the first European convicts and settlers in 1788. These animals were likely to have been a mix of English Thoroughbred and Spanish stock. Only the toughest of horses survived the voyage to the new colony, which could take more than six months to complete. Once in Australia, the survivors had to adapt to a harsh, untamed environment, where they were put to work by the settlers. With further imports, Arab and Quarter Horse blood was introduced. Later, infusions of Welsh Mountain Pony blood—particularly that of a stallion named Dyoll Greylight—were introduced to the breed to produce the smaller Australian Stock Pony. It is said that the versatile Australian Stock Horse is "a breed for every need."

THE FACTS

Origin	Australia
Color	predominantly bay
Height	16.2 hands (1.68 m)
Physique	intelligent, attractive head, long neck, sloping shoulders, strong back and quarters, long, slender legs, hard feet
Features	strong, durable, hardy
Temperament	intelligent, trainable
Use	riding, competition

The Australian Stock Horse is still prized as a working animal. It is most commonly found working on large sheep and cattle farms in the Australian interior.

ANCESTRY

The horses that arrived in the fledgling country with the First Fleet were likely to have been Thoroughbred and Iberian stock.

Thoroughbred
Andalusian
Arab
Welsh Section A
Quarter Horse
Australian Stock Horse

Aboriginal stockmen racing—the indigenous people of Australia are renowned for their horsemanship.

Quarters
Rounded and muscular, nicely sloped

Body
Strong back of medium length, with well-sprung ribs

Head
Alert and intelligent with broad forehead and wide-set eyes

Neck
A good length of rein, well-defined wither slightly higher than croup

Shoulders
Sloping and not too heavily muscled

Chest
Deep but not too wide

Legs
Clean, with broad, flat hocks and well-defined tendons

Feet
Wide at the heel and well-made

A stockman in the Northern Territory rounds up cattle, with the help of a motorcycle outrider.

BRUMBY

In the early 1800s a settler named James Brumby allowed his horses to roam free in the Australian bush. When someone enquired who owned these horses, the answer was "they're Brumby's." The name was to stick, and the horses were to become as much part of Australian fauna as the koala and the kangaroo. The Brumby is a mix of all kinds of breeds introduced to the continent in the early days of European settlement. Those horses that escaped or were set free, bred unchecked, and Australia is now home to the largest feral horse population in the world. They have had a detrimental impact on the natural environment. Australian farmers consider them a pest, as they damage fencing, overgraze cattle pasture, and drink and foul water supplies. Culling programs have been deemed necessary in recent years. In 2000, more than 600 Brumbies were chased and shot from helicopters. Non-lethal fertility control programs have also been tried, while other horses have been trapped and relocated.

The Facts	
Origin	New South Wales, Australia
Color	all colors
Height	varies
Physique	varies
Features	varies
Temperament	a feral breed, the Brumby is generally regarded as too wild to be of use a riding or work animal
Use	wild horse

Brumbies are widespread in the Northern Territory, Queensland, Western Australia, and South Australia. There are scattered populations in New South Wales and Victoria.

Head
This example has quite a fine head, with no coarseness

Coat
All colors and coat patterns are seen

Body
Shapes and sizes vary

Neck
The breed has a tendency to "ewe necks," a conformational defect

Wild Brumbies in Standly Chasm in Australia's Northern Territory

Feet
Generally, Brumbies have extremely hard, good feet as a result of always being on the move

The Brumby has become almost as much a symbol of Australia as the koala and the kangaroo, but numbers must be humanely controlled.

WALER

Named for the first colony of Australia, New South Wales, the Waler is a success story through and through. The horses that arrived with the First Fleet were put to new arrivals, including Thoroughbreds, Clydesdales, Shires, Arabs, and English native pony breeds. But one of the most important influences was to be the Timor Pony from the island off Indonesia, which was introduced for its hardiness, stamina, and agility. The Waler was tough and energetic, and its fast walk and easy canter made it a favorite with the military. With mechanization, however, the Waler fell out of favor and almost became extinct. The Waler Horse Society of Australia has, since 1986, saved enough of the breed to begin a studbook, and today's Waler is popular once more—both as an all-round working horse, and a superlative competition horse. Modern Walers are divided into four categories—pony, light, medium, and heavy.

THE FACTS

Origin	New South Wales, Australia
Color	bay, chestnut, black, brown, bay
Height	16 hands (1.63 m)
Physique	straight head with broad forehead, strong but graceful neck, well-sloped shoulder, deep through the chest and girth, strong back, good legs with plenty of bone
Features	robust, handsome, trainable
Temperament	kind, alert, loyal
Use	riding, competition, harness

New South Wales was the first Australian colony, settled by the British in 1788. It is now Australia's most populous state.

Queensland

Australia

New South Wales

Sydney

Canberra

Victoria

Pacific Ocean

ANCESTRY

The Timor Pony was introduced to Australia in the 1830s by the explorer George Grey, who was later to become the Governor of South Australia.

Thoroughbred
Clydesdale
Suffolk Punch
Cleveland Bay
Yorkshire Coach Horse
Norfolk Trotter
Percheron
Timor Pony
Waler

These Walers display the typically broad forehead that is a feature of the breed.

Back
Medium length and well-muscled

Head
Lean, straight profile, plenty of space between the eyes

Neck
Good length of rein

Chest
Nice and deep, with plenty of heart room

Legs
Exceptionally good and hard, with plenty of bone

Feet
Tough and open, well-defined frog

An elegant chestnut Waler mare and her handsome foal at the Talara Stud, situated in the Lockyer Valley in Queensland, Australia.

184

BASHKIR CURLY

Mystery surrounds the origins of this exotic breed, with its extravagantly curled coat that gives it its name. The original Bashkir breed was found in Bashkiria, in the foothills of the Ural Mountains. These animals were extraordinarily tough, able to survive temperatures as cold as –49°F (–45°C), and particularly adept at finding food under deep drifts of snow. Their thick curly coats protected them against the extreme cold, and could also be spun into cloth. To its owner, the Bashkir was a reliable workhorse as well as a source of milk, meat, and clothing. This extraordinary little horse has found a huge following in the United States, where three horses with peculiarly curly coats were discovered in the Roberts Mountain Range in Nevada in 1898. But how they got there remains a mystery to this day.

THE FACTS	
Origin	Russia
Color	red chestnut, bay, light brown
Height	14 hands (1.42 m)
Physique	large, plain head, short neck, flat wither, upright shoulders, wide body with well-sprung ribs, short legs, hard feet
Features	tough, resilient
Temperament	gentle, biddable, calm
Use	pack, harness, riding

The Ural Mountains form the natural boundary between Europe and Asia. The Bashkir Curly evolved here, in Bashkiria between the Volga River and the Urals.

Head
Rather large in proportion, plain

Back
Broad and strong

Coat
Extravagantly curly and thick

Withers
Low and flat

Neck
Short and quite thick but not unattractive

Shoulders
Upright, leading to restricted paces

There is no accepted explanation of how Bashkir Curly Horses came to be found in North America, but they have found a huge following there. This mare and foal are pictured in Alberta, Canada.

Legs
Strong and clean, good bone

Feet
Small and tough, typical of a steppe breed

As well as their extravagantly curly coats, the Bashkirs also have abundant kinked manes and tails.

BOER PONY

On every homestead of South Africa's Cape Provinces, there is said to be an exceptionally tough little horse trained to be steady to the report of a gun. The Boer Pony is the product of the African veldt: tremendously surefooted, and incredibly hardy—it can carry a man all day, then be content with whatever it can pick from the veldt itself. It has its roots in the Cape Horse and Basuto Pony, with the lean good looks of the latter and the inherent agility of the former. The Boer Pony—which is sometimes called the Boerperd or "farmer's horse"—possesses five gaits, which include the supremely comfortable rack. The breed was almost wiped out by African horse sickness—which remains a killer—in 1870, when thousands perished. Thankfully, a concerted breeding program saved this athletic, hardy breed for generations to come.

THE FACTS	
Origin	South Africa
Color	all solid colors
Height	15 hands (1.52 m)
Physique	lean, straight head, elegant neck, good shoulders, narrow through the chest, medium-length back, slender legs, hard feet
Features	hardy, enduring
Temperament	equable, biddable, kind
Use	riding, harness, endurance, all-rounder

The first horses arrived in Cape Town, South Africa, in 1665. Cape Town is known as South Africa's "mother city." It was colonized by a trader named Jan van Riebeeck, who was on a commission from the Dutch East India Company.

Head
Lean and straight, occasionally showing Spanish characteristics

Back
Tends to be rather short

Neck
Medium-length and well set-on

ANCESTRY

The first horses in South Africa were probably oriental, imported from Java in Indonesia. Persian Arab blood was added and later Andalusian.

Oriental stock
Andalusian
Arab
Hackney
Cleveland Bay
Thoroughbred
Boer Pony

Handsome, agile, and intelligent, the Boer Pony is a breeding success story.

Legs
Slender but well-formed, with good joints

Boer mares and foals pictured at the Iodiona Stud in South Africa. The Boer Pony is used as a utility farm horse and in the popular sport of endurance riding.

Feet
Small and round, tough

MARWARI

From the tips of its delightfully curled ears to its tough compact feet, the Marwari is truly a horse of warriors. It is brave, despite its diminutive stature, and will form a strong bond with its master, to whom it will always be loyal. It is said the Marwari will only leave a battleground in one of three ways: a victor; a savior, carrying its wounded master; or a spirit, having died for him. Indigenous to the Marwari region of Rajasthan, the Marwari is believed to be Arabian in origin, a theory upheld by its elegance and beauty. It was held in great regard by the ruling families and warriors of feudal India—only the royal Rajput families and the Kshatriya warrior caste were permitted to ride the Marwari. It was the surviving Rajput families who saved the Marwari from extinction in the 1930s, and the reason this beautiful equine exists today.

THE FACTS	
Origin	northwest India
Color	all colors, including broken-coated, known as ablak
Height	15.2 hands (1.58 m)
Physique	refined head, curled ears, elegant neck, slightly crested and carried high, well-defined wither, short-coupled, good legs and feet
Features	strong, enduring, athletic
Temperament	brave, kind, loyal
Use	riding, competition

The Marwari breed takes its name from a region within Rajasthan, India's largest state.

Back
Short and powerful, well-sprung ribs and deep loins

Neck
Graceful and well-muscled, stallions showing more crest that mares

Head
Lean and sculpted, sometimes with a slight Roman nose

Ears
Small and neat, extravagantly curled and curving so they meet in the middle

Chest
Not particularly deep, but well-formed

Indian Raghuvendra Singh and Englishwoman Francesca Kelly riding Marwari Horses in Rajasthan. They are the co-founders of Marwari Bloodlines, a group dedicated to the preservation and promotion of the breed.

Legs
Straight and slender, but with good joints and bone; conformation of the hindlegs is particularly important

A Marwari in full dress. The breed is used for ceremonial purposes by sections of the police and the military in Rajasthan.

Feet
Small and open at the heel, very sound

KATHIAWARI

Named for the Kathiawar Peninsula, the part of northwest India that juts into the Arabian Sea, the Kathiawari is closely related to the Marwari. Oriental horses are thought to have been shipped to India by Mogul emperors and there crossed with native stock, the origins of which are not clear. Certainly, the Arabian influence is apparent, both in the breed's elegant appearance and in its affectionate nature. The Kathiawari was bred by wealthy Gujarat families, to whom it was highly prized, and treated much like a family pet. They named various strains after their most prized mares. The breed was also renowned as a warhorse—any horse that could not carry a warrior at speed across open desert would be abandoned; those that survived to breed were the toughest and strongest. Today, the Kathiawari is bred at the Gujarat government stud farms in Junagadh and Innaj.

THE FACTS	
Origin	India
Color	predominantly chestnut, other solid colors except black
Height	15.2 hands (1.58 m)
Physique	chiseled head with some dishing, curling ears, gracefully arched neck, short back, muscular loins, hard feet
Features	robust, hardy, enduring
Temperament	affectionate, but can have an unpredictable temper
Use	military, riding, polo

The Kathiawar Peninsula juts into the Arabian Sea, with the Gulfs of Kuchch and Khambhat on either side. One theory is that a ship carrying Arab horses was wrecked off this coast and the horses swam ashore.

Ears
Curving so they touch in a "scorpion sting" and able to rotate backward to 180 degrees.

Back
Short and strong

Coat
Fine and silky, all colors except black, occasional iridescent sheen

Head
Some dishing in profile

Although the Kathiawari is not a big horse, it is immensely strong and swift, with considerable stamina. It can travel some distance at speed.

Legs
Slender but with flat, dense bone

Feet
Small and hard

The iridescent sheen found in the breed can be seen on this chestnut stallion's coat. His ears illustrate perfectly the "scorpion sting" curve where the tips touch.

FJORD

Norway's native horse is thought to be one of the oldest and purest of breeds. Its links to primitive equine ancestors are clear in its coloring and its upright, black-tipped mane, similar to that of Przewalski's Horse, although it has the 64 chromosomes of the Tarpan, rather than the 66 of the former. It is most likely that horses first came to Norway from southern Sweden and Denmark, where there is evidence of the presence of wild horses since the end of the last Ice Age. Horses were first domesticated in Norway more than 3,000 years ago. The Fjord is thought to be the descendant of those horses. The breed is always dun in color, with five accepted variations: brown dun, the most common; uls (white) dun; gray dun, a misnomer, as the Fjord does not carry the gray gene and is closer to blue dun or grullo; red dun; and yellow dun.

THE FACTS

Origin	Norway
Color	always dun, with primitive markings
Height	14.3 hands (1.50 m)
Physique	refined head, strong, short neck, sloping shoulder, well-defined wither, muscular back, short legs, good feet
Features	strong, robust, hardy
Temperament	kind, gentle, eager to please
Use	riding, harness, pack

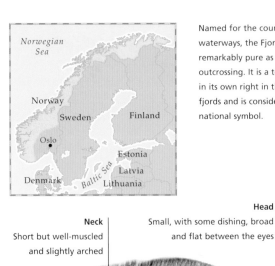

Named for the country's famous waterways, the Fjord has been kept remarkably pure as a breed, with no outcrossing. It is a tourist attraction in its own right in the West Country fjords and is considered a Norwegian national symbol.

Croup
Long, broad, and sloping

Back and loins
Smooth and well-muscled

Neck
Short but well-muscled and slightly arched

Head
Small, with some dishing, broad and flat between the eyes

Mane and tail
Always lighter than the coat color and the mane should stand upright

Shoulders
When used as a working horse, an upright shoulder was desirable, but some sloping is preferred today

The primitive black-tipped, upright mane is shown beautifully by this pretty mare, while her foal's markings have not yet appeared.

Legs
Short and strong, with plenty of hard bone, well-defined tendons and good joints

The Fjord is perfectly suited to the harsh Scandinavian winters, its thick, shaggy coat protecting it from the icy cold. These Fjords have the mealy muzzle also seen in England's Exmoor Pony.

Feet
Hard and sound

ICELANDIC

No outside blood has been added to the Icelandic Horse for some 800 years—horses cannot be imported to the country, and those that leave can never return. There is no Icelandic word for "pony" so the country's native equine is always referred to as a horse. This compact, attractive animal stands no higher than 14 hands (1.42 m). It is thought to have reached Iceland along with the first Viking settlers in the ninth century. The first settlers were followed by new arrivals from Scotland, Ireland, and the Isle of Man who brought their own small horses that mixed with the existing stock. There were few roads in Iceland until just a few decades ago, so the surefooted Icelandic Horse was the primary means of transport on the island. They swam across deep glacier rivers, transported pregnant women to hospital, and carried the coffins of the dead. The Icelandic has a natural four-beat ambling gait, called the tölt.

THE FACTS	
Origin	Iceland
Color	all colors
Height	14 hands (1.42 m)
Physique	neat head, good neck, sloping shoulder, compact, muscular body, short, strong legs
Features	economical to keep, tough, agile
Temperament	docile, gentle, friendly
Use	riding, pack, harness, all-rounder

The Vikings settled in "the land of fire and ice" with their own horses, probably of Germanic descent.

Greenland Sea

Iceland

Reykjavík

Atlantic Ocean

Head
Neat, but can sometimes be heavy

Back
Nicely muscled and proportionate

Croup
Muscular and sloping, high-set tail

Neck
Should be slightly arched, often has a double-sided mane

Shoulders
Sloping

Legs
Forelegs should be straight, hind have some sloping, fetlocks are long

Feet
Strong, dark horn, well-formed

An Icelandic Horse at the Hvita River in Iceland. The country's native breed is hardy and surefooted, ideally adapted to its home.

Two Icelandic stallions play fighting at Schmalztopf Farm in California—the breed has gained worldwide popularity.

DON

The mount of the famed and feared Cossacks, this Russian warhorse was bred for supremacy in the battlefield and was instrumental in driving back the French invasion in 1812. Originally a small, compact horse, the Don was improved and refined with infusions of Arab and Karabakh blood, as well as Turkmene, a breed closely related to the Akhal-Teke. Recognized as the oldest continually bred horse in Russia, the Don shared the nomadic existence of its Cossack masters, roaming in herds and fending for itself—a lifestyle that ensured its tough constitution. The first private studs were established in the eighteenth century, and the Don became the favored military horse not just of the Cossacks but of the entire Russian army. The First World War and the civil war that followed decimated the Don, but it was saved by a government-sponsored breeding program.

THE FACTS	
Origin	Russia
Color	bay, chestnut, gray
Height	16 hands (1.63 m)
Physique	fine head, good length of rein, broad, muscular chest, long back, excellent legs with good bone
Features	hardy, good doer, enduring
Temperament	calm, kind
Use	riding, harness, competition

The Don, a native of Russia, takes its name from the region near the Don River where it has been bred since the eighteenth century.

Voronezh
Russian Federation
Ukraine
Sea of Azov

Head
Typical warmblood head, straight or slightly convex profile

Body
Long in the back, well-sprung ribs, deep through the girth

Coat
Most common colors are chestnut and brown, often with the characteristic sheen of the Akhal-Teke and Karabakh

Neck
Nicely set-on, medium length

Shoulders
Tends to be rather upright, giving the horse a short, choppy stride

Chest
Broad and muscular

ANCESTRY

Persian Arab and Karabakh blood were added to small native Russian horses to increase their size and improve their conformation.

Native Russian stock
Turkmene (Akhal-Teke)
Karabakh
Arab
Thoroughbred
Don

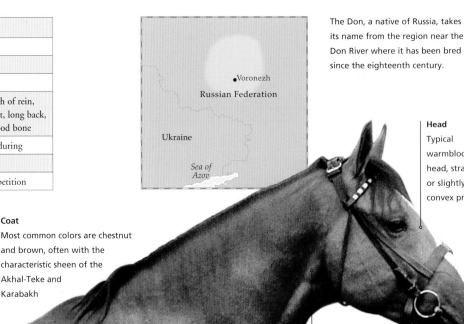

Legs
Efforts have been made to breed out conformation faults such as sickle hocks and calf knees

Arab and Karabakh blood has been introduced to the Don. It can be seen in this handsome horse's refined good looks and gleaming iridescent coat.

Originally bred as a military horse, the Don makes an excellent all-round riding and competition mount.

Feet
Strong and hard hooves

RUSSIAN TROTTER

Overshadowed, somewhat, by the more famous Orlov Trotter, the Russian Trotter was bred to beat the American Standardbred at its own game. At the end of the nineteenth century, imported American trotters were proving much faster than the native breed and the lighter little sulkies—called amerikankas—they drove left the Orlov standing. Attempts to restrict Russian races to Orlov Trotters resulted in more than one ringer, most famously the Standardbred William CK, who raced with false Orlov papers as Rassvet and won 20,000 rubles in prize money. The Russians began to cross their beautiful Orlov Trotters with Standardbreds in a concerted effort to make them faster. The result of these original crosses was a small animal of considerable speed but poor conformation, so they were bred back to more Orlov Trotters and Standardbreds, the type being fixed by the 1950s.

THE FACTS

Origin	Russia
Color	bay, black, chestnut, gray
Height	16 hands (1.63 m)
Physique	light, straight head, long neck, medium-set wither, long back, sloping croup, long legs
Features	fast, tough, fertile
Temperament	quiet, energetic, trainable
Use	harness

The Russian Trotter was widely bred in the former Soviet Union, and raced at tracks in Moscow and St Petersburg. The breeding farms of Telegin and Lezhnev built the foundations of the breed.

ANCESTRY

Although the breed type was fixed in the mid-twentieth century, outcrossings to both Orlov Trotters and Standardbreds continue to correct some conformation defects.

American blood gave the Russian Trotter its superlative speed, while keeping the good looks of its Orlov predecessor.

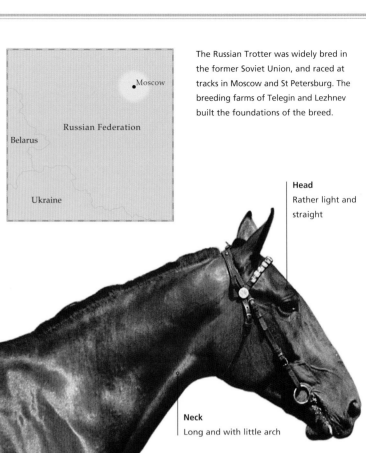

Head
Rather light and straight

Back
Long and somewhat straight

Neck
Long and with little arch

Shoulders
Tends to be rather upright, giving the horse a short, choppy stride

Chest
Broad and muscular

Legs
Strong, with clearly defined tendons, although occasionally sickle-hocked

Feet
Hard and dry, typical of a desert-type breed

The record over the standard harness race distance of just under one mile (1,600 m) is 1 minute and 56.9 seconds. While these trotters are gray, the most common colors for the Russian Trotter are bay, black, or chestnut.

ARDENNES

Julius Caesar praised a breed of heavy horse in his *Commentaries on the Gallic War.* They were, he said, "rustic, hard, and tireless." It is likely that he was describing the Ardennes, the oldest heavy breed in Europe, which has lived on the Ardennes plateau for 2,000 years or more. The knights of the Middle Ages found that these horses could carry them, complete with full armor, unflaggingly into battle. Stoic and apparently fearless, they made superb chargers. Napoleon used Ardennes Horses to pull heavy artillery during his campaigns at the beginning of the nineteenth century. A true coldblooded heavy horse, the Ardennes is nonetheless an attractive creature, which has probably benefited, in recent centuries, from some Arabian blood. Some Percheron, Boulonnais, and Thoroughbred infusions had little effect on the breed, although some Belgian draft blood has given the modern Ardennes a heavier build.

THE FACTS	
Origin	Belgium, Luxembourg, and France
Color	bay, roan, chestnut, gray, palomino; black is not permitted
Height	15.3 hands (1.60 m)
Physique	short, straight head, thickset neck, sloping shoulder, compact body, broad, muscular quarters, short legs
Features	long-lived, strong, surefooted
Temperament	kind, lively, gentle
Use	harness, agriculture, forestry, meat

The Ardennes is a region of rolling hills and dense forest that stretches over parts of Belgium, Luxembourg, and France. The horse of the same name may have lived in the region since the end of the last Ice Age.

Head
Short, with straight or convex profile, broad between the eyes

Back
Compact and strong

Neck
Short and thickset

Shoulders
Nicely sloping for freedom of movement, unusual in a draft breed

Chest
Muscular and deep

Quarters
Wide and well-muscled, broad, sloping croup

Legs
Short and sturdy with strong joints, some feather

Thought to be one of the oldest draft breeds, the Ardennes' history stretches back to ancient Rome.

The broad face of this mare and her foal are typical of the Ardennes, as is the bright bay coloring, which makes for an attractive heavy breed.

BRABANT

William the Conqueror is said to have ridden a Flanders Great Horse—the forebear to the mighty Brabant, or Belgian Heavy Draft—during the Norman Conquest of Britain in 1066. In its turn, it is thought the Flanders was a descendant of the ancient Forest Horse. During the Middle Ages, these massive animals were used as warhorses, able to carry a knight in full armor into battle. Stallions were exported to other nations, but the Belgians were rightly proud of their heavy horse breed and, as a result, it was kept remarkably pure. The Brabant is thought to have provided the foundation for other heavy horse breeds, notably the Shire, Clydesdale, and Suffolk Punch. The studbook for the Brabant was opened in 1855, and the breed was popular, too, in America where a studbook was opened in 1887. With mechanization, the breed went into decline and numbers fell sharply, but a renewed breeding effort at the end of the twentieth century saw a reversal of fortune.

THE FACTS	
Origin	Belgium
Color	red roan, sorrel, chestnut, bay, brown, dun, gray
Height	17 hands (1.73 m)
Physique	small head, short, thick neck, broad chest, compact body, short, hard legs, good feet
Features	powerful, strong
Temperament	docile, biddable, calm
Use	harness, show

Belgium's heavy horse was developed in the West Brabantian region of the country, which includes the capital Brussels.

Head
Small and refined for a heavy breed, although not disproportionate

Back
Short and strong

Neck
Thickset and short

Shoulders
Massive, rather upright

Chest
Deep and broad, muscular

Quarters
Huge and powerful, well-rounded

Legs
Short and exceptionally strong, some feather

The massive Brabant is a superb harness horse. These two handsome specimens are being used for logging in Canada.

Feet
Medium sized and well-made

Right, clockwise from top left: Although a mighty size, the Brabant is still an attractive horse.

A pair of Brabants in harness for a day's plowing.

A Brabant in the snow, Canada.

A Brabant and its owner in Aspen, Colorado—the breed is extremely popular in the United States.

PERCHERON

France's most famous heavy breed owes much to its Arabian ancestors, which gave it its gray color and a surprising amount of refinement for such a massive horse. It is thought that French knights in the Battle of Poitiers of A.D. 732 captured the horses of the defeated, fleeing Moors and used them as outcrosses to their own heavier stock. Further Oriental influence would have been added when Robert, Count of Rotrou, imported eastern horses after the First Crusade of 1092–99. Although its exact origins are unknown, the forebears of the Percheron were undoubtedly used as warhorses during the Middle Ages. In later years, they have served as coach horses, agricultural workhorses, and riding horses. The breed received a further boost when the Royal Stud at Le Pin made Arab sires available from 1760. Two influential Arab outcrosses were Godolphin and Gallipoly, the latter siring the most famous Percheron stallion, Jean Le Blanc, foaled in 1830.

THE FACTS	
Origin	France
Color	gray, black
Height	17 hands (1.73 m)
Physique	handsome, refined head with long ears, long, arched neck, sloping shoulder, broad body, short, strong legs, hard feet
Features	powerful, adaptable
Temperament	tractable, even-tempered
Use	draft, harness, riding

United Kingdom

English Channel

Nogent-le-Rotrou

Bay of Biscay

France

The Percheron is named for the Perche region of Normandy, France, known for its limestone subsoil and lush pasture. Only Percherons bred here may be entered into the studbook.

Head
Attractive, straight profile, with a broad forehead and mobile ears

Body
Powerful and broad

Wither
Prominent

Neck
Muscular and arched, long for a heavy breed

Shoulders
More sloping than generally seen in draft horses

Chest
Broad and deep

The Percheron Dunois, pictured with owner George Pirard in France, the breed's country of origin.

Legs
Short and strong, with as much as 10 inches (25 cm) of bone

A pair of Percherons plowing—the breed's gray color and surprising quality come from its Arab forebears.

Feet
Hard, blue horn, some feathering

BOULONNAIS

Legend has it that the Boulonnais is descended from the horses brought to France from Numidia (present-day Algeria) by Julius Caesar in 54 B.C., as he was preparing to invade Britain. It is sometimes called the "Thoroughbred of the draft breeds," for its elegance, thought to be inherited from Arab and Iberian stock brought to France during the Crusades and Spanish occupation. The Boulonnais was recognized as a breed in the seventeenth century, but there were two distinct strains: the heavy draft and the smaller, swifter Mareyeur, or "horse of the tide." The latter, which had a fast, energetic trot, was used to transport fish from Boulogne to Paris. This type was made largely redundant with motorization, a much faster form of transport, and it is doubtful whether it still exists. Its larger brethren, meanwhile, were all but lost after the Second World War, although a government breeding program ensures the breed's survival.

THE FACTS

Origin	France
Color	gray, chestnut, bay
Height	16.2 hands (1.68 m)
Physique	refined head, short but graceful neck, prominent wither, sloping shoulders, straight back, sloping croup, high-set tail, good legs and feet
Features	powerful, elegant, enduring
Temperament	gentle, quiet
Use	draft, harness

Breeds of heavy horses have been raised in northwestern France since before Christian times. The Boulonnais takes its name from the Boulogne-Calais region. One of the most famous studs was at Eterpigny, near Arras.

Head
Refined and elegant, broad forehead with well-spaced eyes

Back
Broad and straight

Wither
Prominent

Neck
Short and thick, but with a pleasing arch

Shoulders
Muscular and well-sloped

Coat
Silky, polished marble in appearance with delicate skin

Legs
Strong and well-muscled, large, well-formed joints

Two Boulonnais, exercising in the Bay of the Somme, Picardy, France.

Feet
Well-made and sound

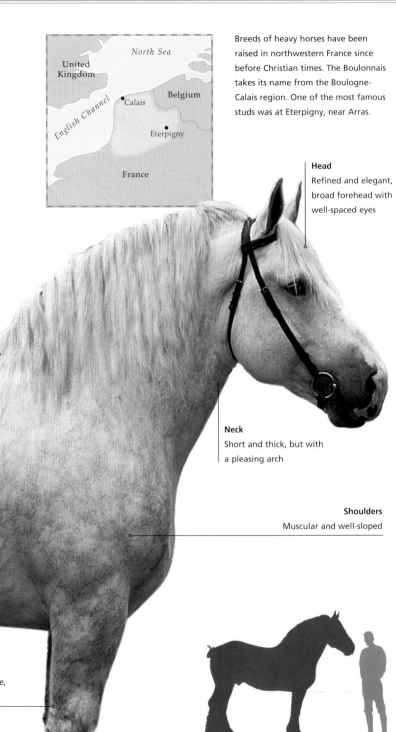

The Boulonnais is both elegant and powerful but has a generally calm and gentle nature.

BRETON

Horses have existed in the mountains of Brittany for millennia, although whether they arrived with the Aryans crossing from Asia or were from Celtic stock, is open to debate. These original mountain horses were hardy animals with an extremely comfortable gait and came to be known as the Bidet d'Allure or Bidet Breton. By the Middle Ages, two types of Breton were being bred: the heavy Sommier, which made a superb pack and all-round workhorse, and the lighter Rossier, more of a riding type. In the nineteenth century, experiments with other stock, including the Boulonnais and Percheron, created a heavier, more powerful animal, suitable for working the plow and light draft work. When crossed with Norfolk Trotter blood, these massive horses produced the Postier, a superlative light draft horse. Today, the two types of Breton remain—the mighty Heavy Draft and the popular, agile little Postier.

THE FACTS	
Origin	France
Color	chestnut with flaxen mane and tail, bay, roan, gray
Height	16 hands (1.63 m)
Physique	neat head, short, thick neck, muscular shoulders, wide, short back, sloping croup, strong legs, hard feet
Features	powerful, energetic, easy keeper
Temperament	calm, willing
Use	light or heavy draft

The Breton takes its name from the region of northwestern France, Bretagne or Britanny, that juts out between the English Channel to the north and the Bay of Biscay to the south.

ANCESTRY

The studbook for the Breton was opened in 1909, for the two separate types. The studbook was closed in 1920, since when no further outside blood has been added.

Mountain stock
Arab
Thoroughbred
Boulonnais
Percheron
Ardennes
Norfolk Trotter
Breton /Postier

The smaller, lighter Postier type of Breton is performance tested in harness and makes an excellent light draft horse.

Body
Broad and compact, plenty of room through the girth

Head
Attractive and proportionate, with a wide forehead and lively eye

Neck
Muscular and powerful, rather short

Shoulders
Long and sloping

Legs
Well-made and strong, plenty of bone

Feet
Of medium size, sound

This three-year-old Breton is an impressive example of the more massive Heavy Draft type, which was influenced by Boulonnais and Percheron blood in the nineteenth century.

HACKNEY

The Hackney has long been prized in England for its unique action and supreme elegance. Indeed, King Henry VIII penalized anyone exporting one of these horses without permission. The name probably comes from the French *haquenee*, a colloquial term for riding horse. But it was as a carriage horse that the Hackney excelled. It possessed great stamina and could eat up the miles with its smooth, ground-covering trot, although without the signature high-knee action at this time. With the flamboyant Regency period (1811–1820) came the demand for more sophisticated carriages, pulled by showy, flashy horses that carried their heads high and proud and lifted their knees with gay aplomb. The Hackney studbook was established in 1883. Since then, the Hackney has been exported all over the world and has helped to found many other breeds. King Henry VIII would have been proud.

THE FACTS	
Origin	England
Color	bay, brown, chestnut, black
Height	15.3 hands (1.60 m)
Physique	refined head, arched neck, long sloping shoulders, deep chest, compact back, level croup, high-set tail
Features	energetic, showy, elegant
Temperament	lively, spirited
Use	harness, riding

The Hackney's spiritual home is probably the county of Norfolk, where the Norfolk Trotter was to play a key role in its development and where the breed registry was originally established. But the Hackney is bred all over England—and the world.

ANCESTRY

An important link in Hackney history goes back to the Shales Horse, a distant descendant of the Thoroughbred Flying Childers. Arab blood was later introduced, but seems to have had little effect

Thoroughbred
Norfolk Trotter
Yorkshire Trotter
Arab
Hackney

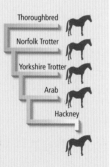

The Hackney has an elegant, refined head, probably due to Arab influence.

Back
Compact, well-muscled

Withers
Low, typical in a harness type

Head
Refined and elegant, sometimes slightly concave in profile

Neck
Long and arched, carried naturally high

Shoulders
Long and powerful, gently sloping

Chest
Deep with plenty of heart room

Legs
Strong, with broad, clean joints. Hocks are set low to allow for greater flexion

Feet
Allowed to grow quite long to enhance the action

A pair of beautifully matched Hackneys in a driving competition— the breed was born out of a desire for flashy, showy carriage horses.

IRISH DRAUGHT

This Irish warmblood is probably descended from the massive Flanders Horses imported after the Anglo–Norman invasion of the twelfth century. Spanish, Connemara, and Clydesdale stock were added, with varying results. The Clydesdale blood was blamed for poor conformation and lack of stamina and Thoroughbred stock was used to correct these faults. The original role of the Irish Draught was as a versatile utility horse, capable of working the land but fine enough to ride and hunt, and smart enough to pull the family cart. The modern version is a good-looking, athletic all-rounder which, when crossed with Thoroughbred blood, produces an exceptional sport horse. However, the Thoroughbred contribution has almost proved the undoing of the Irish Draught, as pure-bred numbers have severely declined.

THE FACTS

Origin	Ireland
Color	all solid colors
Height	17 hands (1.73 m)
Physique	generous, attractive head, high set-in neck, well-defined wither, clean shoulders, powerful back, deep girth, sloping croup, strong legs with clean, flat bone
Features	powerful, proud, robust
Temperament	sensible, kind, trainable
Use	riding, competition, harness

The Irish Draught is bred all over Ireland, although the breed has almost been lost during times of extreme poverty and hardship that have blighted the island. A group of enthusiasts pledged to save the breed and the first branch of the Irish Draught Society was established in County Cork in the 1970s.

Head
Generous, but with no coarseness. Slightly Roman nose is permissible

Body
Compact and deep through the girth, powerful back

Withers
Well-defined

Croup
Long and pleasingly sloping

Neck
Set-in high and carried proudly

Shoulders
Should be clean-cut and not loaded

ANCESTRY

Infusions of Clydesdale blood were blamed for some conformational faults, but these have largely been bred out, with the addition of Thoroughbred lines.

Flanders Horse
Iberian
Connemara
Clydesdale
Shire
Thoroughbred
Irish Draught

Legs
Clean, flat bone, muscular thigh and gaskin

Feet
Well-made and open at the heel, with no boxiness

A perfectly attired hunt follower mounted on a handsome Irish Draught with the Galway Blazers in Ireland.

Laborers returning from the fields with their horse in Ireland about 1900. The Irish Draught was the perfect utility breed.

CLEVELAND BAY

Britain's oldest documented breed is based on the packhorses used in the Yorkshire Dales, known as Chapman Horses. Throughout the Middle Ages, the monasteries of northeast England played an important role in horse-breeding, as pack horses were needed to transport goods between the monasteries and abbeys. But it was the introduction of Barb blood in the seventeenth century that was to have a lasting effect on these efficient compact horses, and to form the Cleveland Bay as it is largely known today—versatile, fast, and good-looking. Latterly, some breeders crossed their Cleveland Bays with Thoroughbreds, the offspring of which came to be known as the Yorkshire Coach Horse, which in turn has played a role in the development of many breeds worldwide. Today, there are still two types of Cleveland Bay: the smaller, which resembles the original Chapman, and the taller Yorkshire Coach Horse type.

THE FACTS	
Origin	northeast England
Color	bay
Height	16.2 hands (1.68 m)
Physique	fine head, long, lean neck, sloping shoulders, medium-length back, powerful quarters, strong legs with plenty of bone, excellent feet
Features	enduring, hardy, agile
Temperament	sensible, honest, intelligent
Use	harness, riding

The breed takes its name from the region of Cleveland, originally "cliff-land," a reference to the cliffs that distinguish the North Yorkshire coastline.

ANCESTRY

Barb blood was vital in the development of the Cleveland Bay, although some Thoroughbred and Arab blood has since been introduced with varying degrees of success.

Chapman Horses
Barb
Thoroughbred
Arab
Cleveland Bay

Although other coat colors do occur, only bay Cleveland Bays may be registered with the English breed society.

Body
Wide and deep, muscular loins and medium-length back

Head
Bold and honest, with kind eye

Neck
Long and lean, well-muscled

Shoulders
Long, deep, and sloping, giving the breed its characteristic straight and free action

Legs
Well-made and strong, 9 inches (23 cm) of flat bone, large joints

Feet
Extremely sound, blue horn

Cleveland Bays were bred to be coach horses and this four-in-hand combination is showing its speed and skill during the cones round of a driving trial.

CLYDESDALE

A Flemish stallion imported in about 1720 by the sixth Duke of Hamilton was to have a lasting influence on the native stock of Lanarkshire, a part of Scotland known then as Clydesdale. The duke allowed his tenants to use his stallion on their mares, and the dark brown horse added substance and height to the local stock. Other local people imported Flemish stock, and in 1808 a two-year-old filly was purchased from a dispersal sale. She was the dam of Glancer, a black colt whose lineage can be found in almost all Clydesdale horses today. Another famous Clydesdale was Baron of Buchlyvie, foaled in 1900 and sold in 1911 for £9,500—a record price for any horse at that time. At their peak, there were about 140,000 Clydesdales in Scotland, with thousands being exported each year. The breed declined with mechanization, although numbers are slowly recovering.

THE FACTS	
Origin	Lanarkshire, Scotland
Color	bay, brown, black, gray, roan, chestnut
Height	16.2 hands (1.68 m)
Physique	handsome head with straight profile, arched neck, sloping shoulders, clearly defined wither, deep body, massive quarters, long legs, sound feet
Features	powerful, elegant, vigorous
Temperament	docile, kind
Use	harness, agriculture, riding

Named for the Clyde River that flows through what is now known as Lanarkshire, the Clydesdale was bred as an all-purpose working draft and was exported all over the world.

Head
Wide forehead, straight profile rather than convex; a white face is characteristic

Body
Deep with well-sprung ribs, strong back

Neck
Long for a draft breed and well-arched

Shoulders
Nicely sloping, giving the breed a flamboyant, flashy action

Quarters
Long and powerful

A striking Clydesdale makes a superb drum horse, combining strength and patience.

Legs
Rather long, but well-made with plenty of bone, silky feather; cow-hocks are acceptable in the breed

A team of Clydesdales working in the Australian bush—the Clydesdale is sometimes called "the breed that built Australia."

Feet
Somewhat flat, but very sound and open

SHIRE

Based on the Great Horses brought to England by William the Conqueror in 1066, the Shire is the largest and most prolific of all England's heavy breeds. These horses added considerable size and substance to native stock, and played a role in the development of an eastern counties type, known simply as the Black Horse. They were dull in color and in personality, but they were improved in the eighteenth century by a Midlands-based breeder named Robert Bakewell and were, for some time, known as the Bakewell Black. The studbook was opened in 1878, by which time the word "black" was a misnomer; the breed was called the English Cart Horse, changed to Shire in 1884. The Shire Horse enjoyed considerable popularity, both in England and in the United States, where the American Shire Horse Association was founded in 1885. Great sums of money changed hands for Shires—during the Great Depression, a good Shire foal was known as "the rent-payer."

THE FACTS	
Origin	Midlands, England
Color	black, brown, bay, gray
Height	17.2 hands (1.78 m)
Physique	long, lean head, long neck, wide shoulders, short, muscular back, wide quarters, long, clean legs, open feet
Features	massive, strong, long-lived
Temperament	gentle, kind
Use	harness, agriculture, riding

These heavy horses were bred primarily in England's "shire" counties of Derbyshire, Leicestershire, Lincolnshire, and Staffordshire. Flemish Horses were imported in the early seventeenth century to help drain the fens of Lincolnshire and may have played a role in the development of the Shire.

Head
Long and lean, often with a Roman or convex nose

Neck
Well-arched and long for a heavy breed, carried proudly

Back
Short and strong, not dipped or roached

Quarters
Long and sweeping, wide with plenty of muscle

Shoulders
Deep and wide enough to carry a collar

Chest
Deep with plenty of heart room

British breweries once relied on the mighty Shire to transport beer, and many breweries still retain these glorious horses for show and tradition.

Legs
Forelegs should be straight, hindlegs set in line with quarters with broad hocks; a good 11 inches (28 cm) of flat bone

The Shire makes a magnificent coach horse—despite its size, it is surprisingly agile.

Feet
Open at the heel, round and well-made, plenty of silky feather

SUFFOLK PUNCH

"A leg at each corner" is an equestrian term that could have been coined to describe the Suffolk Punch. A stout little horse, it is thought to be the oldest heavy breed in Great Britain, going back to the sixteenth century. All Suffolk Punches today can trace their lineage back to one stallion, Thomas Crisp's Horse of Ufford, foaled in 1768. He was described as a bright "chesnut"—this spelling is correct when used to describe the Suffolk Punch—short-legged and large-bodied. This type of heavy breed was well-suited to working the heavy clay of East Anglia in the east of England. However, the introduction of the tractor, at least as well suited to the flat East Anglian terrain, dealt a severe blow to the horse population of the region, with just nine foals being born in 1966. Since then, efforts have been made to restore the breed, but it is still listed as critical by the Rare Breeds Survival Trust.

THE FACTS	
Origin	England
Color	chesnut
Height	16.3 hands (1.70 m)
Physique	small head, thickset neck, low-set shoulder, deep girth, short back, powerful quarters, short legs, good feet
Features	early-maturing, long-lived, tough
Temperament	gentle, active
Use	harness, show

The heavy clay of Suffolk, Norfolk, and Essex required a horse that was strong, with wide, open feet and little feather. The Suffolk Punch's comparatively small size belies its immense strength.

Head
Comparatively small with a broad forehead

Body
Large in relation to the legs

Coat
Always chesnut, in seven recognized shades ranging from pale to deep red

Quarters
Rounded and massive, very powerful

Neck
Short and thickset, powerful

Shoulders
Set low, muscular

A Suffolk Punch working a potato field in Suffolk, England. There are only 300 of the breed left in the United Kingdom.

Action
For a heavy breed, the Suffolk Punch has a lively, active trot

Legs
Hindlegs are set close together, legs are short and very strong

The Suffolk Punch is always chesnut—by tradition spelled without the middle "t"—and has a small, refined head for a draft breed.

JUTLAND

There is some debate as to whether the Suffolk Punch influenced the Jutland, or vice versa. Certainly, there are similarities, although the former is more refined that the latter. A stallion named Oppenheim LXII, thought to be a Suffolk Punch, was imported to Denmark in 1860 and had a considerable influence on the development of the breed. Six generations later, the stallion Aldrup Menkedal, considered the foundation stallion of the breed, was born. Almost all Jutland Horses can trace their lineage back to Hovding and Prins af Jylland, two of his sons. Since 1928, Jutland Horses have been used by the Carlsberg brewery of Copenhagen to haul its drays—the brewery at one time kept 210 horses. Today, however, it retains about 20, which take part in shows, festivals, and films, promoting both the beer and the breed.

THE FACTS

Origin	Denmark
Color	mostly chestnut with flaxen mane and tail
Height	16 hands (1.63 m)
Physique	large, blunt head, broad, flat wither, short neck, compact body, short legs, powerful quarters
Features	enduring, sturdy, active
Temperament	docile, willing
Use	harness, agriculture

Heavy horses have been bred on the Jutland Peninsula of Denmark since the Middle Ages, and there has been considerable trade between the English and the Danes for centuries, including the import and export of horses.

ANCESTRY

During the eighteenth century, Frederiksborg blood was introduced to improve the paces of the Jutland, and later Cleveland Bays and Yorkshire Coach Horse lines were added.

Suffolk Punch
Frederiksborg
Cleveland Bay
Yorkshire Coach Horse
Jutland

The Jutland shares similarities with England's Suffolk Punch, but its rather blunt head lacks the elegance of the latter.

Back
Short and wide

Head
Comparatively small with a broad forehead

Neck
Short and thickset, powerful

Shoulders
Deep and wide enough to carry a collar

Chest
Deep with plenty of heart room

Legs
Short, with large, rather fleshy joints, coarse feather

Sturdy and attractive, the Jutland is still used as a heavy draft breed in its native Denmark.

Feet
Open and well-made, sound

FINNISH UNIVERSAL

Finland's only native breed is known as the Finnish Universal for its all-round capability. It is said to fulfill every need that might be required of a horse, from agricultural and light draft work to trotting and riding. The Finns are rightly proud of this celebrated horse, which is perhaps the most versatile and fastest coldblood in the world. It is known that there were horses in Finland in the Bronze Age but the breed's exact origins are unclear. It was used extensively by the Finnish army and may have been crossed with imported foreign breeds. However, since the studbook was opened in 1907, no further outcrossing has been permitted. The studbook has since been divided into different sections for the breed's different uses: the lighter riding type, trotting type, draft type, and pony type. Finland's national horse is universal indeed.

THE FACTS	
Origin	Finland
Color	predominantly chestnut but most solid colors are seen
Height	15.2 hands (1.58 m)
Physique	well-shaped head, strong neck, powerful shoulders, muscular quarters, clean legs with little feather
Features	strong, active, swift
Temperament	kind, willing, docile
Use	harness, riding, agriculture

The Finnish Universal was used extensively in the fields and forests of Finland, as it is agile even in heavy snow and over rough terrain. Today, the country holds regular work championships for its native breed.

Head
Well-shaped and not over-large

Body
Somewhat long, but well-muscled

Quarters
Powerful and muscular

Neck
Short and strong

Shoulders
Can be rather upright

Ever popular in its home country, there are thought to be about 20,000 Finnish Universal Horses today, with around 1,000 foals born every year.

Legs
Generally well-made and very sound, with a little feather

Action
The Finnish Universal has an active, fast-stepping stride

A Finnish Universal at work raking hay for the coming winter. Until recent decades, a good horse or two was essential for every Finnish farmer.

226

NORTH SWEDISH

Sweden's draft breed is descended from ancient native Scandinavian stock. While it lacks the size of the heavier coldbloods, its neat and compact frame made it supremely suited to the forestry and lumber work for which it was originally bred. Although stallions stand at only around 15.2 hands (1.57 m), the North Swedish is remarkably strong and has considerable stamina. It is one of the world's most rigorously guarded and tested breeds, with strict regulations regarding breeding being introduced in 1903, although the studbook was not opened until 1909. Horses are routinely x-rayed to ensure no conformational faults are bred in, and are tested on their pulling power and fertility. Particular attention is paid to their obliging and amenable temperament, for which the breed is renowned. The modern North Swedish is still used for logging and by the country's military, who prize it for its durability and economy.

THE FACTS	
Origin	Sweden
Color	all solid colors
Height	15.2 hands (1.57 m)
Physique	pony-like head, short, crested neck, sloping shoulder, deep body, rounded quarters, short legs
Features	powerful, robust, economical keeper
Temperament	willing, obliging, even-tempered
Use	forestry, pack, military

Horses are thought to have existed in Scandinavia for several thousand years. The North Swedish is principally bred at the Stallion Rearing Institute at Wangen, where it undergoes vigorous testing to ensure that the high standards of conformation, strength, and character are upheld.

Head
Comparatively small with a broad forehead

Neck
Short and thick with some crest, broad at the base with broad, low wither

Back
Wide and long with sloping croup and low-set tail

Quarters
Long and sweeping, wide with plenty of muscle

Shoulders
Muscular and sloping

Chest
Notably wide and deep

Legs
Short with good bone and broad joints, some feather

Feet
Round and solid

Smaller than most draft breeds, the North Swedish has a pony-like head and neat, compact frame.

North Swedish Horses race over the frozen Aare Lake in Sweden—although a draft breed, its speed and agility make it highly suitable for trotting.

RUSSIAN HEAVY DRAFT

A relatively young breed, Russia's coldblood was started in the 1860s in Ukraine at the state studs of Khrenov and Derkul, using local mares put to Ardennes stallions. It was introduced to the equestrian cognoscenti as the Russian Heavy Draft at the Paris Exhibition of 1900. Other blood was introduced, including Brabant, Percheron, and Orlov Trotter, this last giving it considerable quality and freedom of action. It was almost eliminated by the First World War and the subsequent Russian Civil War, but enough stallions were left to revive and continue the breed. As well as light draft and agricultural work, the breed is used to produce a fermented milk drink called kumys, which was considered a great tonic by the literary giants of the nineteenth century, including Alexander Pushkin and Leo Tolstoy.

THE FACTS	
Origin	Russia and Ukraine
Color	chestnut or roan
Height	14.3 hands (1.50 m)
Physique	refined head, medium-length neck, deep chest, low wither, broad, long back, sloping croup, short legs
Features	long-lived, fertile, strong
Temperament	gentle, willing
Use	light draft, agriculture, harness

Developed at the state studs of Derkul and Khrenov, the Russian Heavy Draft is now bred in several Russian locations as well as in Ukraine and Belarus.

ANCESTRY

As recently as the 1920s, the Russian Heavy Draft was sometimes referred to as the "Russian Ardennes," as it was based predominantly on Ardennes stallions.

- Ukrainian stock
- Ardennes
- Brabant
- Percheron
- Orlov Trotter
- Russian Heavy Draft

Back
Long, with long, sloping croup

Neck
Muscular and crested, sometimes rather fleshy

Shoulders
Strong and well-sloped

Chest
Broad and deep, well-muscled

Legs
Short and sturdy, forelegs set well apart

Action
Unusually for a draft breed, the Russian Heavy Draft has an excellent ground-covering walk and cadenced trot

Feet
Medium-sized and in proportion, some light feather

A Russian Heavy Draft pulls a farm cart in its native land.

Pictured at a state stud farm in Russia, this playful foal already shows the quality of the fine horse it will become.

230

SCHWARZWALDER KALTBLUT

Known as the "pearl of the Black Forest," the Schwarzwalder Kaltblut is a striking horse descended from the native coldbloods that have inhabited the region since the Middle Ages. The breed was developed using Noriker and Haflinger blood, and it shows the influences of the two. Infusions of Brabant lines to increase height largely failed. The farmers of the Black Forest region, reluctant to use these unsuccessful outcrosses advocated by the breed association and studbook, continued to breed to native stallions and gave the resulting animals falsified papers. By the early part of the twentieth century, the authorities allowed breeders to use whatever stallions they wished. There are now almost 50 state-approved stallions, and some 700 registered mares, in Germany. The modern Schwarzwalder is an active, nimble horse, with a happy disposition and striking coloring.

THE FACTS	
Origin	The Black Forest, Germany
Color	sorrel to dark chestnut with light mane and tail
Height	15.2 hands (1.58 m)
Physique	quality head, arched neck, low wither, sloping shoulder, short back, compact body, strong legs
Features	surefooted, agile, strong
Temperament	willing, good-natured
Use	agriculture, forestry, harness, riding

The Black Forest comprises a wooded mountain range in Baden-Württemberg in southwest Germany. The region's farmers needed an agile, surefooted horse that was also capable of considerable pulling power. It is now bred at the state-owned stud at Marbach.

ANCESTRY

Sometimes known as the Schwarzwalder Fuchs, or Black Forest Chestnut, the breed is thought to have inherited its striking coloring from the Haflinger.

Native German stock
Noriker
Haflinger
Brabant
Schwarzwalder Kaltblut

Body
Compact and strong with short back and sloping croup

Coat
The most popular color is deep chestnut with a dappled pattern on the rump and silver mane and tail

Head
Refined and attractive, wide forehead and tapering to the muzzle

Neck
Muscular and arching, proportionate, low-set wither

Shoulders
Powerful and heavily muscled, nicely sloped

Chest
Broad and deep

Legs
In proportion to the body, strong and well-made, good joints and little feather

Feet
Medium-size, well-shaped and sound

The head of the "Black Forest Chestnut" is full of quality—it is an exceptionally beautiful horse for a coldblood.

Well-matched Schwartzwalders pulling a sled in Marbach, Germany; the striking coloring is typical of the breed.

232

Glossary

action The way a horse travels and the movement of its legs at various gaits. It includes the carriage of its head, neck, and tail. The desired action for a horse varies by breed and discipline.

amble A slow, lateral pacing *gait*.

biddable Easily led, taught, or controlled. Docile and obedient.

bloodline The ancestry of a particular horse.

bone The measurement around the leg just below the knee or *hock*. This measurement can help determine the horse's ability to carry weight.

boxy foot A narrow, upright foot with a small *frog* and closed heel.

breed A group of horses bred selectively for consistent characteristics over a long period. Horses recognized for each breed are entered into an official *stud book*.

broodmare A female horse that is used strictly for breeding. They are usually chosen in hopes of passing down their outstanding attributes or desirable ancestry.

cannon The large, sturdy bone in the foreleg that is located between the knee and the *fetlock*. The equivalent bone in the hindleg is the shank.

carriage horse A horse especially bred or trained for drawing carriages.

coldblood The name used to describe the heavy European breeds of horse descended from the prehistoric Forest Horse. They often have calm temperaments.

colt A male horse under four years of age that has not been castrated.

conformation The overall body shape, size, and proportion of a horse. Good conformation means that a horse has a desirable physical build. Bad conformation means a horse may be predisposed to injury, or be uncomfortable to ride.

cow-hocked A fault in *conformation* in which the hocks of the hind legs turn inward like those of a cow.

croup The area along the horse's hindquarters from the highest point down toward the tail.

desert type A horse bred in desert conditions or descended from such desert stock. They are resistant to heat and can survive on little water.

dished face A concave facial profile as exemplified by the Arab horse.

dorsal stripe A dark line running down the back of a horse from the base of the mane to the base of the tail. This is a *primitive* marking found on horses with dun coloring.

draft horse A heavy, large-boned horse bred for pulling or carrying large loads and farm work.

easy keeper A horse that maintains a good weight without having to be fed extra supplements or rich feed.

eel stripe see **dorsal stripe**

equine Of or relating to the family *Equidae*, encompassing horses, donkeys, zebras, and other species now extinct.

ewe neck A conformational defect in which the neck appears to be the wrong way up, curving outward on the underside and inward—concave— on the top.

extravagant action High knee *action*. It is greatly prized among harness horses.

feather Long hair on the lower legs. Often seen in heavy draft breeds.

fetlock The lowest joint in a horse's leg, just above the hoof.

forage Any food eaten by horses, such as pasture and hay.

forelock The mane growing between a horse's ears that falls on the forehead.

frog A shock-absorbing wedge-shaped pad in the sole of the hoof that contacts the ground first with each step.

gait A pattern of repetitive foot movements used in locomotion, including the walk, trot, and canter.

gelding A male horse that has been castrated.

hand A traditional unit of measure for horse height, equal to 4 inches (10.16 cm). When a horse height is given with a dot, it is to indicate inches in addition to the number of full hands, not a decimal fraction of a hand.

harness Equipment used on a horse to permit it to be driven or to pull a carriage, rather than be ridden.

heart room The measurement taken around the horse's barrel just behind the front legs. Good heart room suggests that a horse will have enough heart and lung capacity to stand up to strenuous exercise.

heavy horse Any large draft horse.

hock The joint in the center part of the hind legs, equivalent to the human knee.

hotblood The name used to describe horses having ancestors that trace to Thoroughbreds or Arabians. Generally they exhibit fine bones, fine, thin coat, and high energy.

length of rein The neck in proportion to the rest of the body. A horse with "good length of rein" has a neck nicely in proportion to the body, not too short, and well set on the shoulders.

light horse A horse other than a heavy or draft horse that is suited to riding or carriage work.

mare A female horse over four years old.

mealy muzzle A light browny-gray muzzle, like that of the Exmoor Pony.

Oriental horse A horse originating from Central or West Asia, including the Arab and Barb.

outcross The mating of unrelated horses; introduction of outside blood to a breed.

pacer A horse that employs a two-beat lateral *gait* in which it moves both right feet and then moves both left feet. A pacing horse moves its head side to side to counterbalance the way its feet move.

pack horse A horse that is used to carry a load or burden in a pack as opposed to being a riding or carriage horse.

palomino A golden-colored horse with a light or white mane and tail.

piebald Coat color of black and white patches.

pony A small horse measuring 14.2 hands (147 cm) or less.

primitive A horse that exhibits characteristics associated with the primitive horse breeds, such as the Tarpan and Przewalski's Horse.

pure-bred A horse with pure bloodlines that has and can produce the physical characteristics required of its breed.

quality Overall degree of refinement in a breed, usually due to Arab or Thoroughbred influence.

quarters The rear part of a horse's body from the rear of the flank to the top of the tail down to the second thigh of the leg. Also called the hindquarters.

Rare Breeds Survival Trust A U.K.-based organization committed to the preservation of endangered breeds of farm animals.

skewbald White coat with colored patches, any color other than black.

sport horse A horse especially bred or trained for dressage, jumping, eventing, or endurance.

stud An establishment where animals are selectively bred.

stud book A genealogical register of horses maintained by a breed society.

topline The line from the back of the *withers* to the end of the *croup*.

tractable Easily managed and trained.

warmblood A half-bred, or part-bred horse resulting from a cross between a hotblood breed or type and a coldblood breed or type.

well-sprung ribs Long, rounded ribs giving ample room for heart and lungs and well-suited to carrying a saddle.

withers Point at the bottom of the neck usually characterized by a slightly raised area just above the shoulders. A horse's height is measured from the ground to the withers.

INDEX

ACKNOWLEDGMENTS

Weldon Owen would like to thank the following people for their assistance in the production of this book: Bob Langrish and Sue Stimpson.

PHOTOGRAPHS

Key t=top; l=left; r=right; tl=top left; tcl=top center left; tc=top center; tcr=top center right; tr=top right; cl=center left; c=center; cr=center right; b=bottom; bl=bottom left; bcl=bottom center left; bc=bottom center; bcr=bottom center right; br=bottom right

AAP = Australian Associated Press Images, ALA = Alamy, AniP = Animal Pictures, AUS = Auscape, BA = Bridgeman Art Archive, BLa = Bob Langrish, BM = British Museum, CBT = Corbis Traditional Licensing, GI = Getty Images, iS = istockphoto.com, MP = Minden Pictures, PUB = Public Domain, REU = Reuters Pictures, SH = Shutterstock, TPL = Photolibrary

Front cover BLa; **front flap** BLa; **1**bc, br, bl, br BLa; **2**c GI; **4**c AAP; r GI; **6**br CBT; bl GI; tl TPL; **7**br AUS; **8**c TPL; **12**cl CBT; bl iS; **13**br GI; tl TPL; **14**tc AUS; bl, tr GI; cl, tr iS; b, cl MP; **15**tcl, tl GI; **16**tc, tr, tr, tr BLa; tc CBT; tr TPL; **17**tl, tr BLa; **18**bl ALA; br, c GI; bl SH; tr TPL; **19**bc, bl, tl BM; br CBT; tr GI; **20**br BA; 20-21 b, bc, tr GI; bl TPL; **21**cr CBT; bc, cl, tl GI; br iS; **22**cl PIC; b, br, cl, tr TPL; **23**bl, br, tl, tr GI; **24**br GI; b, t TPL; **25**tl, tr GI; bc SH; **26**b CBT; bl iS; tr TPL; **27**bl CBT; bc, br, tl, tr GI; **28**bc, tr GI; bl PUB; cl TPL; **29**c GI; **30**bc, br, tr CBT; cl PIC; **31**tl ALA; tc, tr CBT; bc GI; bc TPL; **32**bc, bl, cl BLa; **33**b, bc, br, br, br BLa; **34**br BLa; bl TPL; **35**c BLa; **36**bl, br BLa; **37**c GI; **38**br BLa; bl GI; **39**c CBT; **40**br BLa; bl CBT; **41**c TPL; **42**bl, br BLa; **43**c TPL; **44**bl, br BLa; **45**c BLa; **46**bl, br BLa; **47**tl CBT; tr SH; c TPL; **48**br BLa; bl TPL; **49**c BLa; **50**br BLa; bl TPL; **51**c BLa; **52**br BLa; **53**cc TPL; **54**bl, br BLa; **55**cc BLa; **56**br BLa; bl TPL; **57**tl BLa; tr CBT; bc TPL; **58**br, br BLa; bl WIKI; **59**cc BLa; **60**br BLa; bl CBT; **61**cc CBT; **62**bl, br BLa; **63**cl, tr BLa; **64**br BLa; bl SH; **65**cc BLa; **66**bl, br BLa; **67**cl, cr TPL; **68**bl ALA; br BLa; **69**br ALA; cl, tr BLa; **70**bl, br BLa; **71**cc CBT; **72**br, cl BLa; **73**bl, tc BLa; br CBT; **74**br BLa; bl SH; **75**cc BLa; **76**br BLa; bl iS; **77**cc BLa; **78**br BLa; bl CBT; **79**br, tc BLa; **80**br BLa; bl GI; **81**cc AAP; **82**br BLa; bl CBT; **83**br, cl, tr BLa; **84**br BLa; bl TPL; **85**cc BLa; **86**br BLa; bl CBT; **87**tl BLa; tr CBT; bc, br GI; **88**bl, br BLa; **89**cc, tl BLa; **90**bl AniP; br BLa; **91**cc BLa; **92**bl, br BLa; **93**br, tr BLa; cl TPL; **94**bl, br BLa; **95**cl, cr BLa; **96**bl AniP; br BLa; **97**cr AniP; bc, tl BLa; **98**br BLa; bl TPL; **99**tl, tr AniP; bc BLa; **100**bl, br BLa; **101**bc, br, tl, tr BLa; **102**bl AniP; br BLa; **103**cc BLa; **104**br BLa; bl CBT; **105**br, cl BLa; tr SH; **106**bl, br BLa; **107**bl, br, tr BLa; tl CBT; **108**bl, br BLa; **109**cl, cr BLa; **110**bl, br BLa; **111**cc BLa; **112**br BLa; bl TPL; **113**cc BLa; **114**bl ALA; br BLa; **115**cc AniP; **116**bl, br BLa; **117**cc ALA; **118**bl, br BLa; **119**cc TPL; **120**br BLa; bl GI; **121**cc BLa; **122**br BLa; bl CBT; **123**cc BLa; **124**bl, br BLa; **125**cc BLa; **126**bl, br BLa; **127**bl, tc GI; br TPL; **128**bl, br BLa; **129**tr CBT; bc, tl GI; **130**bl, br BLa; **131**cc BLa; **132**bl, br BLa; **133**bc BLa; br, tc CBT; **134**br BLa; bl SH; **135**cc BLa; **136**bl, br BLa; **137**cc BLa; **138**bl, br BLa; **139**cc BLa; **140**bl, br BLa; **141**cc BLa; **142**bl, br, br BLa; **143**cl, cr BLa; **144**bl, br BLa; **145**cc CBT; **146**br BLa; bl TPL; **147**tl CBT; cr iS; bl TPL; **148**bl, br BLa; **149**cc TPL; **150**bl, br BLa; **151**cc BLa; **152**bl, br BLa; **153**br, tr BLa; bl, tl TPL; **154**br BLa; bl CBT; **155**br, tr BLa; tl CBT; **156**bl, br BLa; **157**cl, cr BLa; **158**br BLa; bl TPL; **159**cc BLa; **160**bl, br BLa; **161**cc BLa; **162**bl, br BLa; **163**tr GI; cc TPL; **164**b, bl BLa; **165**cc TPL; **166**b, bl BLa; **167**tc GI; bc TPL; **168**b, bl BLa; **169**cc CBT; **170**bl, br BLa; **171**cc BLa; **172**b, br BLa; **173**cc TPL; **174**br BLa; bl TPL; **175**br, tl, tr BLa; bl TPL; **176**bl, br BLa; **177**bl, tl, tr BLa; br TPL; **178**bl, br BLa; **179**bc, tl, tr BLa; **180**b BLa; bl CBT; **181**cc CBT; **182**b BLa; bl GI; **183**cc BLa; **184**bl, br BLa; **185**cc BLa; **186**b, bl BLa; **187**cc TPL; **188**b, bl BLa; **189**cc BLa; **190**bl, br BLa; **191**cc BLa; **192**bl, br BLa; **193**cc CBT; **194**b, bl BLa; **195**cc BLa; **196**b, bl BLa; **197**cc GI; **198**b, bl BLa; **199**cc SH; **200**b BLa; bl REU; **201**cc REU; **202**b BLa; bl iS; **203**cc TPL; **204**b BLa; bl CBT; **205**br, tl BLa; bl GI; tr iS; **206**b BLa; bl CBT; **207**cc BLa; **208**bl ALA; b BLa; **209**cc CBT; **210**bl, br BLa; **211**cc CBT; **212**bl, br BLa; **213**cc AniP; **214**br BLa; bl GI; **215**cc BLa; **216**b BLa; bl GI; **217**cc BLa; **218**b BLa; bl CBT; **219**cc iS; **220**b, bl BLa; **221**cc TPL; **222**b, bl BLa; **223**cl, cr BLa; **224**b, bl BLa; **225**cc CBT; **226**bl TPL; **227**cc TPL; **228**b, bl BLa; **229**cr GI; **230**bl AniP; b BLa; **231**cc ALA; **232**b, bl BLa; **233**cc PUB; **235**cc GI; **239**bc, br, br

ILLUSTRATIONS

Argosy Publishing, www.argosypublishing.com 16b, 16c, 16cr, 16cl; **Andrew Davies/Creative Communication** 12tr, 14cr; **Ian Jackson/The Art Agency** 14–5; **Guy Troughton** 12c, 12tc, 12tl, 12tc, 12cr, 12br, 12bc, 13bc, 13bc, 13tr.

MAPS & GRAPHS

The Breeds section 34-233: locator maps by **Damien Demaj**, ancestry infographics by **Andrew Davies/Creative Communication.**